Confessions of a
CLOSET EATER

Jackie Barrile

Tyndale House
Publishers, Inc.
Wheaton, Illinois

Scripture quotations are taken from *The Living Bible*, © 1971 Tyndale House Publishers, and are used by permission of the publisher.

Third printing, Tyndale House edition, August 1984

Confessions of a Closet Eater
Library of Congress Catalog Card Number 83-50238
ISBN 0-8423-0438-X, paper
Copyright © 1983 by Jackie Barrile
All rights reserved
Printed in the United States of America

*Dedicated
to my wonderful husband, Ron.
He never doubted my love for him,
nor my need to recover—for me.
To my blessed son, Jeff—
for the unconditional patience
and understanding
he constantly gave to me.
And to all my courageous girls
for allowing me to share in their pain
and subsequent growth
through that pain.
I love you all,
and I thank God for you.*

CONTENTS

FOREWORD

I had been in the weight-loss ministry for just a few months. I sat in my living room with a lovely thin woman wondering, *What in the world could you possibly want from me?* After getting acquainted and exchanging small talk with her, I asked the question, "Pat, what can I do for you today?"

She began to reveal her story. I could identify closely. She had been 279 pounds—a little heavier than I had been, but not much. She had wanted to lose weight, and so had I; she had called out to God for an answer, very similar to my own experience. But there the similarity ended. I had sought out a small group and begun a Bible study to find the help and support that I needed. I even tried intestinal bypass surgery that left me in fragile health—and still fat as well. It was through the support of close friends and the application of biblical principles that I experienced victory at last.

Not so for Pat. She had achieved what she called "stolen" victory. "It is all false," she told me. "My victory is a lie."

I couldn't understand what she was saying. "How so, Pat? What do you mean your victory is a lie? I can see from your picture that you are at least 120 pounds thinner than you were. This is a miracle, I can see that for myself."

She looked at her picture, and then began to cry as she confessed, "It's not a miracle. I do not have victory. I have stolen my thinness and given the glory to God, but I can't do it anymore. I can't stand the guilt and condemnation any longer. Please, Neva, will you help me?"

"I'll try, Pat, but you must explain what you are talking about."

"Do you know how I have lost weight? I have learned to throw up."

"You what?" I had never heard of such a thing.

"You heard right. I didn't stop eating—I just learned to throw it up after I ate. It's so awful, Neva, it's almost worse than being fat. At least then I didn't have any secrets and the fear that someone would find out. But now, someone is bound to find out because I can't stop throwing up even after I eat a normal amount. I've lost enough weight, and my husband says he doesn't want me to lose anymore, but now I can't stop. I'm afraid I will die. I'm so scared, Neva. And the worst part is that I've been telling everyone that this is a miracle that God is doing for me. And he isn't! I did it myself, and now it is worse than before I ever began. I need help and I need it now!"

I didn't know what to say to this most precious sister. Was her method of weight loss any worse than the things I had tried—clubs, pills, fad diets, and the extreme of having my small intestine shortened? The goals my new friend and I had were the same. Only our "solutions" were different. The shame of my having to have that type of surgery was equal to that of my friend sticking her finger down her throat.

But how could I help her? I couldn't understand her total problem. But what I did understand, I shared with

10

her. I shared Scripture and prayer, and she went on to the Overeaters Victorious program. Eventually she got better and found the power and desire to control her weight responsibly, but it took a long time and I felt so inadequate to help her.

I was not even aware that this condition had a name. I had never even heard the word "bulimia" and did not hear it for at least a year. By then, Pat was so much better that she had dared to become pregnant and gave birth to a healthy baby. We praised God that he spared her morning sickness, which could have triggered old habits.

I began to earnestly pray, "God, give someone this ministry." I prayed that this someone would help by sharing her experiences in a book. This would not only help the "Pats" but those like myself who want to help them.

I thank God for Jackie Barrile and her book, *Confessions of a Closet Eater*. There have been many bulimic sisters as well as anorexic friends in Overeaters Victorious groups. We are one, we are sisters, encouraging and accepting one another as children of God. But we have needed this book. We have needed Jackie Barrile. We thank God for her.

I have been helped and ministered to by this book. If you presently have in your life bulimic habits, anorexic thought patterns, or are tired of overeating binges, I highly recommend this book.

Thank you, Jackie, for helping us. All of us—your overeating sisters and brothers—gratefully thank you.

Because of Jesus,
Neva Coyle

Confessions of a
CLOSET EATER

ONE
CLOSET EATING

And so it begins again. Why can't I stop? Why don't I try? Why do the contents of the refrigerator seem to call *me* alone? It's building now, the familiar excitement that only huge amounts of food can satisfy. Forget willpower, forget that I promised myself not to do this again. Blood is pounding in my head. I can see the food sliding down my throat, so smooth and soothing. The refrigerator door is open now. My friend and accomplice, food, awaits me. Mounds of it in every shape and color.

If I pop the cinnamon rolls from the freezer into the microwave, they should be ready by the time I polish off the hamburger and French fries I bought on the way home. I'll devour them quickly so there'll be time for the remains of the Mexican dinner I fed the family last night. Have to hurry, though, or the rolls will get cold. Hurry, hurry! I can't get enough, fast enough. This calls for at least half a bottle of ketchup.

Mmmmm, delicious. With a stick of butter and the last of the strawberry preserves, the rolls are superb! If I don't keep eating, the nausea will stop me—so I'll have some cold cereal with lots of sugar. And don't forget the stale cookies.

Here I am again, standing at the kitchen counter stuffing everything in sight into my mouth. Nothing is more degrading. Part of me is appalled by what I'm doing. But I can't do anything to stop myself from binging like this. It's as if I'm outside my body watching myself gorge. One moment I'm furious at myself, and the next I'm engulfed in the ecstacy of consuming more and more. Sometimes I want to cry out for help. Yet I'm terrified that someone would hear me. What if I'm interrupted before I've had my fill? I can eat 40,000 calories at a time. Luckily, the kitchen is strictly my domain. Neither my husband nor my son even ventures in for a glass of milk. No one ever notices that I've picked the refrigerator clean again.

The guilt and aching are beginning to set in. Terrible gas pains are wracking my bowels with agonizing spasms. I feel disgusting and look worse. If I'm trying to commit suicide, there must be a cleaner way.

Dear God, I'm scared. The cramps are worse than ever. My back aches and my stomach has begun to throb. Have I gone too far this time? What will I tell the doctors if I end up in the hospital? Certainly not the truth—*anything* but the truth.

I'll just lie down by the toilet and hope it all passes quickly. But I know it will take time. You see, I've tried vomiting but am unable to do so. No amount of pressure in the throat will rid me of the now-congealed garbage; so I take laxatives which don't work for hours.

My family will be home soon. What excuse should I give this time? I can't always be coming down with a cold. I hope the fact that I'm sick again won't spoil their evening. How can I keep subjecting them to this? Well, it's not as if I'm ever going to do this again. I'm an adult. No sir, this is absolutely the last time, *finis*, over.

Whom do I think I'm kidding? After five years, my

binges are becoming more and more frequent, sometimes even three or four times a week. The depression always starts well in advance. Even when I'm eating normally I dread the inevitability of the next gorge. Soon I begin to feel I'm unworthy of my family's affection, so I avoid them altogether and act silent and morose.

By now my body feels like it's been hit by a truck. The thing I dread most, the terrible gas, has set in—wracking my lower body with spasms of pain and odor. Even my eyes are swollen. No need to try getting clean, as the diarrhea will go on for hours, probably all night. I feel as though the smell of discharged gas is even in my hair. How could I do this time and time again?

People are dying horribly of cancer, children starving to death in various parts of the world, and at my house a very insecure woman is gorging for the umpteenth time. What possesses a person of normal intelligence to stuff herself with food, only to purge herself with laxatives afterwards?

Tonight I decide to take a sleeping pill and go to bed early with the hope that I'll be unconscious when the worst of the pain strikes. No such luck. Every hour on the hour I'm up and in the bathroom again. By morning, however, most of the throbbing has stopped. I feel guilty, disgusted, anesthetized. Also, not hungry. The diarrhea usually lasts about two days, and everything I eat within that period will go right through me, so I'll be able to zip up my pants again soon. What a relief!

I'm really going to get a hold of it this time! Never again! After all, I'm an adult. I run a household and have responsibilities. I can deal with it—I know I can.

Sound familiar? If so, you too have a condition known as "bulimia." The symptoms are hard to ignore. Number one: They demand absolute privacy, for obvious reasons. It's one thing to make polite conversation over a steak dinner. But tamping down a chocolate cake with a quart of ice cream—eating until the only thing I feel is physical pain—requires total concentration.

Then comes symptom number two: Having achieved my goal, I do a complete reversal and try to get rid of everything. How? If I were lucky, I could go straight to the toilet and vomit. However, I am not that fortunate. I have to rely on laxatives to wash my "sins" away. This means hours of terrible bloating, pain, nausea, and the pungent smell of gas. Doctors will tell you it's good if you can't vomit, as this is even more detrimental to your health than taking laxatives. However, to a fellow bulimic, it is disastrous. How long can you deceive your family with contrived illnesses?

Gorge—purge—bulimia.

This is not exactly the kind of affliction I can point to with pride; so along with thousands like me, I have become a closet eater. We eat after coming home from work, during lunch breaks, and whenever our families turn their backs.

It isn't easy to write about something I'm so ashamed of doing. It frightens me that someone I know or love will read this and think even less of me; but I don't believe anyone could do anything more to me than I'm doing to myself. By going public, I'm hoping that someone, anyone, suffering right now from a binge will know he or she is not alone. People care; I care!

In order to come out of the "closet," in sheer desperation I confided my secret to my family. At first they were shocked; but shock turned into disbelief, disgust, impatience, and finally a disguised disenchantment. The only help they were able to offer me was that of a watchdog or keeper. That made it a game. How to successfully sneak a binge. What a challenge! I must say, I was certainly up to it.

During a short TV commercial, I can manage to wolf down all the dinner leftovers and half a loaf of bread. If I'm really quiet, I can also polish off a bag of pretzels or potato chips, and reclaim my seat in front of the TV. Yet I manage to have nary a crumb on my face, not a telltale sliver of evidence stuck in my teeth! It is actually becoming almost child's play. Of course, as the winner of the game, I get the prize; a complete evening of unadulterated pain and torment. The disease of the year—it's not.

Sound dumb? Not if you're "one of us." You see, no one can keep me away from food. (Sorry, family.) In order to survive, the dirty stuff must be faced three times a day. It's fuel, a necessary factor to human existence. Unfortunately for a lot of us, it is being abused and mischanneled as we use it to satisfy our inner conflicts, instead of to fill our stomachs. We distort the hunger pang by stripping it of its validity. I demand food not only to satisfy my physical hunger, but to fill my emotional needs as well. Food becomes a baby-sitter, tension releaser, emotional painkiller, and keeper of all the responsibilities I don't want to handle. Am I getting any closer?

I can go back to my childhood for clues as to why and how it started. But as a very self-centered woman, I have a tendency to wallow in the past and lose all perspective. The point is to stop binging, not dwell on what can't be changed. Being engulfed in self-pity and guilt will accomplish nothing but more of the same. I can't speak for you, but I'm tired of throwing myself and anyone else I can blame into a self-made pit I can't climb out of—all the while wracking my brain to figure how to get the refrigerator into the pit with me.

I've known I needed help for some time. (It usually

occurs to me about 5 o'clock in the morning after a binge.) I also knew I couldn't help myself. I had tried too many times before. My first attempt was to keep a diary of everything I ate. (During a binge, I actually ran out of space.) Hypnosis was attempt number two. It only masked the real reasons behind the eating. I hid behind suggestions to myself, instead of facing the real issues. You name the cure, and I've tried it!

So before asking someone else for help, I decided to get a few things straight in my mind. First, did I really want help? Affirmation came through loud and clear. Next, I must admit to what I am doing; to recognize that it is destroying my mind and body, as well as wreaking havoc on my family. My *mind*, because going on a binge is a totally self-centered act which doesn't allow my brain to deal with anything considered disturbing, or a threat from the past or present. My *body*, because it is very hard on the digestive tract; not to mention the effects of prolonged laxative use. Then there's the distraught family to be considered. They suffer too. I'm depressed, physically sick, and usually very withdrawn. I'm unable to explain my feelings, and the habitual cycle of gorge-purge continues.

The depression begins well in advance of the binge. I start dreading the inevitable even when I'm eating normally. I know it's only a matter of time before I stumble and start the destructive cycle all over again. Then withdrawal. I crawl into my own world of guilt and degradation.

* No longer worthy of my family's affection and attention, I would avoid them altogether if I could. Instead, I'm silent and morose, quietly hating this thing in me that refuses to be controlled. Observing this behavior, they're left wondering what they've done to deserve such treatment.*

I am withdrawn, and can't discuss the cause of the

withdrawal. How can I if I don't understand the reason myself? I know only to seek further refuge by the means available. Unfortunately, my refuge is my next fix—a binge. I'm lashing out against the world and myself; every cookie I eat is an attack, each candy bar a pathetic thrust, a futile gesture at best. My binges are a desperate attempt to both hide, and to reach out for help. Gorge—purge—bulimia. . . .

TWO
DIZZY, SICK, DISGUSTED

Every word you've just read was written during one of my typical binge-purge attacks. This was the dawn of truth that was to help begin my recovery. Finally, I had actually captured a cycle on paper! For the first time in five years I was able to partially wake up from one of my bad dreams. It was not enough to make me stop yet, but enough at least to—make me watch! By seeing and feeling a binge and purge at a time other than during the cycle itself, I could experience my nightmare while more fully awake. Suddenly it was a challenge I could live with. I knew it wasn't practical to try to eliminate the cycles immediately, but it was enough just to understand and grow through them for awhile. In the examination of the entire cycle I could watch it grow and also probe for reasons as to the intensity, and then de-fusion, that always signaled relief and release. With my mind and eyes wide open, I would no longer be prey to the mindless onslaught of bulimic tyranny. Each attack would wear a number that would never have to be repeated!

By choosing pen and paper as weapons, I could react constructively for a change. After what seemed a lifetime of binging and purging, facing the honesty of my writings seemed not only tolerable, but cleansing as well. I had never reconciled myself to the hideous gorging, nor to the subsequent purging.

From that moment on I was to rest a little and grow a lot. Pen and paper became my faithful companions, as the truth was transferred again and again from my head to my hand. Therapy was seeing my disorder flow from the fearful darkness of my mind into the hopeful light of my honesty.

If I could capture the cycle itself, could I also isolate the urgency of the onset, or the moments just prior to the cycle?

For me, the horror of binging lay in the mindless trance that would envelop me time and time again. I was constantly crossing over the line of reality—across my kitchen threshold, and into the unreality as if I were stepping on a land mine. I'd enter the kitchen on a harmless errand, maybe to jot down a needed item on the shopping list, or to get my son a glass of water, and BOOM! Suddenly the kitchen was transformed into a huge, airy playpen. Bright and shiny toys were lying everywhere—in the refrigerator, on the counters; every cupboard housed a surprise all mine for the taking!

At first it's so exciting! I'm a child again at the beginning of a dream. I want all the toys at one time. I'm absorbed and captivated by the textures, colors, and tastes. The more I eat, the more I want. I wish this ability to have it all, this freedom, would never end! As a child I am released from all responsibility; there is only the freedom of the food and me. This wonderful twilight sleep is such a relief. No pain—my mind is finally numb and relaxed. I can't remember anything that happened in the past or might happen in the future—I'm only alive in the now. As a child I don't have a schedule, clocks don't exist—time is standing still. The playpen is my safe retreat, my protection. No one can hurt me as long as I stay here, in the now—in my own world. I don't want to share this world with anyone. I want to enjoy it all by myself.

A child doesn't have to achieve her playtime, she doesn't have to win it or deserve it—it's hers, unconditionally, just because she's a child.

I'm so absorbed in my toys, I don't notice that the playpen is becoming confining; and the more I play, the more confined I feel. My stomach is beginning to hurt, my eyes are swelling, and my head hurts. This isn't supposed to happen. I'm sick, and the sleepy comforting fog is beginning to lift, forcing me to be more aware of my surroundings. The sides are closing in and I can't see out anymore. Maybe if I eat faster, play harder, I can ward off the oncoming entrapment; but the sides continue moving in and I'm feeling hot, suffocated, panicky! The drowsiness of my vision is turning into an uncontrollable nightmare, only now I'm much more awake! The baby in the playpen is changing also; a trapped and frightened animal is emerging from a cage. The bright and shiny toys are losing their flavor. Their soft and freeing shapes are becoming piercing weapons that in my period of adjustment from sleep to wakefulness I can't seem to ward off. The confines of my cage won't allow escape!

I'm dizzy, sick, and disgusted! That reflection was never an innocent child, it was a grotesque red and purple pig! A dirty, filthy animal that's too stupid to be tamed! She's evil and deserves to be hurt, tortured, hated for her lack of self-control. She's big and fat, and I hate her!

O dear God! When did my vision of sugarplums become the nightmare of my destruction? When did my playpen turn into a cage? When did my innocent and happy child become a raging and smelly beast to be hunted and destroyed?

THREE
PLEASURE
AND PAIN

A binge by any other name is still a binge. Spraying an entire aerosol container of whipped cream into my salivating and puckered mouth, gasping all the while for precious air in between hurried gulps, was a definite indication of an appetite gone awry.

However, identifying the satisfaction I was deriving from my mindless gorging was quite another matter. By writing the account in the preceding two chapters,* I had pinpointed what it felt like, but I still didn't understand how to deal with it. I felt a release. But from what, and why was the release necessary in the first place? I would have to wait for other binges, to receive other answers. More binging . . . then, I'd had it! I was housing an active and very angry, erupting volcano in the middle of my stomach. Why was my body betraying me like this?

The only thing I knew for sure was this: Every time this eruption took place, my confused mind sent out the same warning signal—*acute hunger!* I'm not

*The first of which was later published in the *Ladies Home Journal.*

talking about a sandwich or a couple of cookies. I'm talking about an insatiable appetite that had nothing in common with a friendly hunger pang. Somehow, eating when already full allowed a release and relief that was necessary to keep my secret.

I tried to explain my release theory to my husband, Ron—being careful not to "share" the purge phase, of course. But he had difficulty in taking my "theory," or my "appetite," seriously. Especially since I kept losing weight. I finally reached him with an example he couldn't ignore: "Ron, you know the release you feel from making love? Well, while it's true gorging doesn't produce a climax (please forgive my bluntness), the heightened senses, the oblivion to everything and everyone around me, the total release—is the same." Needless to say, that got his attention!

Most of the bulimics that I counsel today share this same feeling while in what I call the "playpen" phase of the binge. It isn't until they come to see the hideous "cage" that this oblivion becomes a torturous nightmare.

I, myself, did not feel the same "freedom" from purging that I did from binging. For me, purging was my impatient and quick way to get rid of the condemning and very painful results of the binge. Purging itself was difficult and painful.

I also had the feeling that I was punishing myself somehow for committing such a vile "sin in the first place. My body would already be in tremendous pain from the "junk" ingested, but it was never enough. I wanted to physically abuse that "stupid child" even more. Why didn't "she" ever listen to me! If she was so determined to hurt herself, then I'd really give her something to hurt about!

One woman (for the sake of her privacy I'll call her Nellie) was taking up to 120 laxatives at a time. Because of her addiction to them (and in order to feel completely "flushed" after each binge), she had been driven constantly to increase the dosage. Nellie's doctor told her that if she had been a woman of forty-two, instead of twenty-two, she probably would have died. More than once Nellie felt death would have been preferable to the excruciating pain experienced each time she purged.

So guilt-ridden, sick from the food swallowed, and in acute desperation, it was hard for her to see any other alternative. Crying because of horrendous leg cramps, she was scared to death. Because there was nothing left in her system for her body to "empty" itself of, her body was literally "emptying itself." Nellie was trying to get rid of calories. Nellie was trying to punish herself—but punish herself for what?

While waiting calmly for friends one afternoon, I became a little "nervous." I decided I needed a "quick fix," so I attacked one loaf of bread, a cake, and pint of ice cream. I actually broke every blood vessel around my eyes trying to vomit about 40,000 calories in fifteen minutes. I was panicky, in a lot of pain, and furious! I knew I couldn't wait for my faithful laxatives to take hold, so I locked the bathroom door and did my thing. I emerged looking like I'd been in a fight... and lost. I had two bloody, almost black eyes, and I was so exhausted I had to lie down for a couple of hours. I don't know what my company did; I didn't answer the door.

Many who vomit don't even have to stick their finger down their throat. They have learned to cause the stomach muscles to contract automatically. Others find throwing up so easy, it's hard to keep even "safe" food down. However, for many, vomiting isn't easy. They must resort to shoving their whole fist down their throat; and if that doesn't work, they try a fork, spoon, or stick. Obviously, it's very, very dangerous.

A lovely woman of thirty-five was convinced she could stop the vomiting any time she wanted to—she just wasn't ready to give it up yet. (For her a binge might consist of five lettuce leaves; she ate only to have something in her stomach to throw up.) The bathroom door became jammed one day, and she couldn't gain access to the toilet. Becoming enraged, she tried to kick the door down, slamming her fist again and again into the wall, and crying uncontrollably for an hour or more. Until this time, she had never acknowledged her addiction to her release, her need for the purge. Thinking it was just a residual "bad habit" that she could break when she chose, she was more tired of the vomiting than frightened of it. She was actually experiencing a bulimic cycle without the benefit of her crutch! Finally, she knew what it felt like to go into the "cage" and see it for what it really was! It was a real step toward recovery.

For this woman and others, binging is the punishment. In the beginning stages of recovery, food is their weapon. It is a way to punish themselves for what they can't as yet say or even get in touch with. These women depend on vomiting as their release; the binging is usually more difficult to accept, but the purging is ecstasy.

What would create such an explosive compulsion for me and so many others? Where did all the anger during the "cage" phase of the binge or purge come from? I could understand being mad at myself for the "mindlessness," but I sensed it was much more. If an active volcano indicates a building pressure and subsequent eruption of hot and angry lava, then could my lava represent feelings? Feelings I thought I was successfully handling? Was I, in reality, only hiding from them? If so, when did it start? Could it be that the pressure of these emotions was, in truth, the catalyst for their eruptions? Wanting to be optimistic,

I wondered if it were possible to cool the lava a little, somewhere between the pressure and the actual eruption.

Perhaps I wouldn't feel so threatened if I knew my feelings could be cooled, if they could be understood a little better before they were felt, exposed, and dealt with. If I were ever going to rescue that child from her playpen-masked cage, I would have to identify the nature of my volcano—once and for all.

FOUR
THIS IS
A RECORDING

We are born with a perfect computer—our minds. A tape began recording on this computer the minute we were born, hence the beginning of memory. When I began "digging," I was surprised to discover how far back I could actually remember. But more than that, I was surprised at how much *control* my "tape" had over me—just by virtue of its nonstop recording and playing. Even though I can't actually recall lying in a crib with my foot stuck in my mouth, I know my memory was busy storing away everything going on around me, and *to* me. I believe I was much more aware of my surroundings than I ever understood. So, if anything and everything were being recorded on a tape in my mind, then my personality was already being molded.

Doctors tell us that as early as four years of age a person's character is already formed. This certainly correlates with Rita, a woman I have been counseling for about a year. Her earliest recollection is that of passing in front of a mirror and thinking, *You're the ugliest and fattest person I have ever seen and I hate you.*

Now, at four years old, she probably wasn't aware of pretty, ugly, fat, or thin! Yet somewhere on Rita's "tape" this very negative "fact" of her selfimage had been recorded, and was to be played back over and over for twenty anorexic and bulimic years.

The tape I had been listening to simply repeated my childhood as I had perceived it, again and again. I heard it not necessarily as it really happened, or the way others remembered it happening—but from my childish point of view. When I began to sort through my memories, I realized that I was still a captive audience listening and obeying what the tape was playing, only now I was an adult.

My father was, and is, a very strong-willed man. To me he never seemed to be wrong. So to question him was wrong and futile. If I didn't agree with him, it was I who didn't "fit in," or feel accepted by him. I wanted so desperately to get his stamp of approval. I needed him to validate my existence. Even though I knew what displeased him, I was never sure what did please him. I was always left feeling I had somehow fallen short of the mark. Instead of learning who I was, I was busy trying to learn who he wanted me to be. But never getting an answer. He would say, *Be your own person,* but I wanted very much to be his little girl. I became frightened because I could never be perfect, as he seemed to be.

My father's education hadn't gone beyond the seventh grade, and yet to me, he had a master's degree in common sense. There didn't seem to be anything he couldn't figure out or accomplish. Rather than chance his disappointment by my failures, I decided very early never to put myself in a position in which I might fail him. I became frightened to try anything. I wanted to show him my strengths, not my weaknesses. If I couldn't show how smart I was, I could show him how strong I could be in my feelings.

31

I would try never to cry in front of him, never to show disappointment, anger, or resentment. I withdrew into myself as much as possible, thinking somehow that would please him. All the while my tape was recording, *Don't try, you'll only fail. Don't feel, you'll only expose your weaknesses and fail again.*

I remember one night as I was preparing to go out on a date, I was very nervous. Dad told me, "Just be yourself, honey," and he walked out of the room. I'll never forget the helplessness I experienced that evening. *Just exactly who am I, Dad? Please come back and tell me. Am I a naturally happy person? Am I moody? Do I have a sense of humor?* I felt very, very lonely and very, very dumb.

I was so busy feeling stupid and trying to hide that stupidity from Dad, and yet afraid to talk to him about it for fear of his rejection. I know beyond a shadow of a doubt that he would have been more than willing to alleviate my feelings of inadequacy where he was concerned, but I was too afraid. I didn't stop to analyze my feelings, I was too occupied with hiding from the feelings. I wish I had taken the risk; my tape would have been a much more positive one.

My thirteenth year also stands out in my mind. It was the first time I had a real boyfriend. When he broke up with me after three months, I was devastated and felt rejected. When I told my mother, she sympathized with me and told my father. I was hurt and embarrassed to think the boy didn't like me anymore, and I didn't know where to put these strange new feelings. Dad watched me for the better part of an evening and then said, "If I thought a good spanking would get you out of this mood, I'd give it to you."

BOOM! To me, that indicated loud and clear, you don't expose rejection. If you do, you are a weak person. Strong people don't expose negative feelings.

Without realizing it, I made up my mind that I would never again show my feelings.

That is what my tape recorded, and that is what my tape replayed later. In hindsight, I know what Dad was really saying, but didn't communicate. It was: *"Your mother tells me that some boy has hurt you. You are my little girl, and if I could, I would feel the hurt for you, but I can't. If I thought it would do any good to give you a good shaking to help you realize there will be many, many boys in your lifetime, I'd do it.*

What happened? We simply didn't communicate. Neither of us told the other our true feelings. If I had said, "Dad, I'm hurting and don't understand rejection. Please don't you reject me too, or try to take away my right to feel it," I know he would have explained himself, and we could have really talked. But I didn't. Instead, that scary tape just kept recording and playing back.

I imagined I was stupid, that my opinions, point of view, and feelings were foolish and to be kept to myself. I decided this at an early age, which meant that my very perfect computer reproduced that tiresome "tape" without my ever questioning it for the first thirty years of my life. It didn't matter what Dad or anyone else told me; I heard only *my* "truths."

Consider Sandy. Her father was constantly comparing her with her friend at school. No matter what grade Sandy brought home, her dad's comment was, "That's nice, but how did Jan do?" Jan was a better student; Jan always did better. Sandy's computer was busy recording this continuous feedback for the better part of her childhood. Its constant repetition told her, *No matter what grade I bring home, Jan will bring a better one.* In her adult years, this repetition became, *No matter what I do, someone can and will do it better, so why should I try?*

33

When, as a grown woman with children of her own, Sandy confronted her father with her remembrance, he was shocked. His memory recalled the grade comparison very differently. Jan was an abused child. Her mother was an alcoholic who, because of her condition, couldn't give Jan affection or reassurance. They were a very poor family because the father never worked and the mother couldn't. Neither one had an education, nor the inclination to get one. Jan was determined to have enough schooling to be a lawyer and "grow" out of the repressive atmosphere of her home.

Sandy's father, knowing all of this, was very much interested in her progress, and wanted to see her succeed. Sandy was also aware of Jan's home life, but saw only the comparison being made between Jan and herself. Her dad never explained why he asked about Jan, because he assumed Sandy understood. Sandy saw only that she could never get as good a grade as her friend and thus could never please her father. She devoted the rest of her school years to trying to please him instead of pleasing herself. If only they could have communicated to one another, her tape might have recorded and repeated very different and positive feelings toward herself in her future life.

Just recognizing the misconnection between herself and her father was an enormous help for her. Today they enjoy a much closer and more communicative relationship. This is not to say that all "tapes" are misconnections. Many women have suffered very real abuse in their childhoods. But that doesn't mean that for the rest of their lives they must relive those tapes with every person or situation that arises.

I realized that in order to begin my recovery, I would first have to look a little closer at my "tape" and pinpoint "key" recordings. I needed to get a more enlightened view of how these tapes from my past were affecting my now, and influencing my future. If parts of them were misconceptions due to misconnections, I needed to recognize them as such and create a new, more positive tape. As long as I continued to listen and believe the old tape, it would forever dictate my todays and predict my future. If I listen and believe a tape that says I was stupid, then I am stupid now and will be stupid tomorrow, so why try?

While I can't erase these "hauntings" from the past, I can understand that what I have been hearing played is a *lie*. Thus, I am capable of creating a new and truthful tape of my choice. I also have the choice of believing the lie or the truth.

This is one of the first steps I ask those I counsel to take. Usually they have been hearing lies in their heads that serve to convict them before they've even allowed themselves a trial. I ask them to believe me when I tell them that what they have been listening to is a lie. The truth is, they are capable of getting better, and they will.

You are not an evil person who is unworthy of love. To believe that is to believe a lie. Choose not to believe it; choose to discover how the bad tape was created, and commit yourself to creating a new tape that discredits the erroneous one.

My computer was created to be my slave, not my master. It's purpose is to help me, not condemn and enslave me. I can say to it, *That's a lie, and I choose not to accept it any longer. Thinness will not insure my happiness, nor will it bring acceptance and love from others.* I had to be willing to see the lies and misconceptions, and dare to tell myself, *That's simply not true.* Then I started creating a new, more productive and optimistic tape.

Every time my tape said, *Jump!* I had asked, *How high?* I was very tired of blindly obeying. Enough!

It's time to take back your own leadership role. The mind must be the helper as intended, and we must become the boss for a change—and for good!

FIVE
BEAST IN THE
BEAUTY

I have seen and heard many horror stories connected with bulimia. To go into great depth to describe them here would probably serve no purpose except to heap even more guilt on the already stoop-shouldered bulimic.

I remember all too clearly the woman who swallowed a metal spoon while vomiting and had to have it surgically removed. But she went for help only after a three-day settling period—because she had swallowed the spoon *before* successfully "getting rid" of about 50,000 calories (50,000 is equivalent to over thirteen pounds of edibles). Needless to say, she was a very sick woman.

A sixteen-year-old girl died in the bathroom choking to death on her own vomit. There are many, many more casualty accounts. But when I was in a bulimic cycle, all the fears and threats in the world didn't keep me from my playpen, my cage.

I rarely stepped over that "threshold" with the intention of eating everything but the kitchen sink! I was nearly always going to have just a few of the prettier "toys." The awful guilt and fear would never hit me until the playpen had become a cage. But by then I was only conscious of gorging to put off feeling the guilt and fear. I didn't want to think about what was to follow—my flight into fantasy and my journey into the pit.

When not in the cycle I was easily scared by my body's physical reactions to binging and purging. I felt like a selfish, horrible mother to risk the possibility of dying and take the risk that my son go the rest of his life without knowing why. He might wonder if it was his fault, if he had somehow asked too much of Mom, or whether he was such a terrible son I couldn't stand raising him anymore. It goes without saying that I was not the helpmate, friend, or lover of my husband's dreams.

My life was consumed with fear, guilt, binge, purge. A vicious cycle of cycles.

So to threaten me with the possibility of death, or put the fear of God into me by reassuring me of my continual "sinning," only drove me deeper into the nightmare.

Naturally, when a person's body is constantly being forced to digest huge quantities of food, most of it containing high dosages of sugar, there are going to be both negative and harmful reactions. I can't say what long-range effects bulimia will have on its victims; I simply don't know. Having been involved with the illness for less than ten years, I am not qualified to speculate or diagnose. I am a recovered bulimic, not a doctor. However, I can and will share the physical side effects I have thus encountered in myself and others.

Which came first, the chicken or the egg? This is the question many are asking about bulimia. People like me are either hypoglycemic or at least border-line. Is this a result of the high intake of sugar during a binge? The "yo-yo" syndrome of either gorging or fasting might produce low blood sugar at times. Or is it vice versa—are the gorging and fasting a result of hypoglycemia? Which came first? I don't know; but I do know we are plagued with both. We also have difficulty in knowing when we're "full." Back to the chicken-and-the-egg theory. I don't know if this lack of discernment is a result of our abusing the "full" signal (coming from the stomach to the brain) to such an extent that we no longer recognize the signal, or if the connection between stomach and brain is defective in the first place. Only time and the medical community can give us the answers.

However, other side effects have not been as elusive: hair loss and dry skin due to vitamin deficiencies, diarrhea, and a loss of the menstrual cycle. When away from the "yo-yo" aspect of bulimia, many find the menses start again; others never do.

I have seen girls who have had their teeth capped as many as three times due to the high acidic content of the vomit. Two girls I know have had much of their stomachs removed. Many suffer with a constant hoarseness and perpetual sore throat, and others who have become "hooked" on laxatives are now unable to go to the bathroom without them. Though no longer binging and thus feeling the need to take them, they have found it more comfortable first to slowly cut down on the amounts being taken. They feel their bodies are thrown into too much of a shock if they try to quit "cold turkey." A few still have to take some "helpers," but most eventually have been able to discontinue laxative abuse. The longer they have been submitting their bodies to this abuse, the harder it seems to permanently go off of the crutch.

I discontinued their usage years ago, and I pray that I'll never feel forced to take another one!

SIX
A GLIMPSE
OF TRUTH

One of the most perplexing emotional symptoms of bulimia is a distorted body image. I saw myself as FAT, and no matter what others told me they saw, I didn't believe them. It was as if I carried a fun-house mirror around in my head that only I could see. When I looked into a "normal" mirror, my distorted image would flow from my vision and reflect back at me. Everyone else was wrong; I had to believe my own eyes, didn't I?

A young woman I was counseling once a week came to me one day in absolute amazement. I had been talking with her for about two months—and in that time, I could not help her to see how thin she really was. In her eyes, there was no such thing as too thin; she was sure everyone else was much thinner. She had been to the market that morning; and upon leaving she noticed a lovely, "thin"girl reflected in the windows of the market. She did a double take as she always did when competition was around, and couldn't believe her eyes. The girl in the reflection was herself!

She was the very attractive and thin woman. She

had finally caught a glimpse of the truth others had been trying to show her. Before, her own eyes could only reflect the distorted image she had put there. This glimpse was enough to cause her to doubt some of the other ideas she had been living with and believing. It was a beginning. . . .

SEVEN
I'M A WOMAN

While it's true *my* perceived childhood was not always an accurate barometer of the facts and feelings of those involved—that should not and must not invalidate the accuracy of the "tape" being played in the minds of many.

A case in point: Ruth lives with her parents and loves them dearly. However, she has always shrunk away from her father's touch. She thinks, *It must be me. Dad is a wonderful and generous man; yet, when he looks at me, I feel dirty, like he's looking at me sexually. I know I'm a terrible person to think that about my father, but I can't help it. I don't even like to be in the same room with him if we're alone. I'm uncomfortable and will think of any excuse to leave. I know it's all in my head. I'm ashamed of myself. I know it means I'm a filthy witch to harbor such dirty thoughts about my dad, but I can't even wear my nightgown around him without feeling like I'm tempting him. Naturally I haven't told Mom. How could I? She'd probably throw me out of the house for such evil thoughts. Am I possessed? What's the matter with me? Just thinking about it makes me hungry.*

It was a relief for Ruth just to be able to put her thoughts into words without feeling judged and sentenced an unworthy daughter and an evil woman. However, she still didn't trust her interpretation of the tape that was being constantly replayed in her mind, and she needed to know if what she was "feeling" was accurate or not.

With her permission, I spoke with her mother, hoping she could offer some insight and valuable input. Ruth's mother was able to share that the father did have sexual feelings for young girls; however, he had never put those desires into action, and had been seeing a counselor. Because of his weakness, he was deathly afraid, both for and of his own daughter. Ruth's feelings, her perceptions of the situation were correct. She was sensing his fears, his shame, and feeling dirty herself. Ruth is now trying to understand her father better, and even sympathizing with him. His fear of being dirty does not mean *she* is! It's his weakness, his trial, not something she has to absorb and carry for the rest of her life.

Sarah remembers the day her dad told her it was her fault her male cousin had tried to undo her blouse because she had teased him by being too friendly.

What does "too friendly" mean at age eight? Why was he normal and I "sinful"? I felt dirty and unclean. I was always careful after that to be completely "covered," and I learned to contain my smiles to noncommittal grins. Later, when boys began looking at me, I still felt dirty, like a piece of chocolate cake that was going to make them fat and grotesque! I went out of my way to avoid being "feminine." I felt somehow in cahoots with the devil, just by virtue of my sex! Men are legitimately conquering the world and trying to stay clean while "I, the harlot" am forever driving a wedge between them and their decency. I have to work with them all day long, and I can't wait to come home and throw up!

When Sarah reexamined her tape of the incident, she didn't feel as ashamed as she had; but she did feel angry. Looking back, she was furious with her dad for being so blatantly judgmental of her "little girl body," and for being so wrong! Through the years she had begun to believe all men saw her body as evil and shameful. It was hard for her to turn to God to end her torment, because in her mind he was also a man and therefore just as condemning of her femininity. God, Dad, and all men became the enemy, constantly judging her a "flirt" and an "instrument of the devil."

Sarah's mother had left her father for another man early in Sarah's childhood. He judged all women to be the same, including his own daughter. Sarah is trying to see that by finding all men guilty, even God, she is trapped in her dad's judgment. It is taking time, but Sarah is creating a new tape that says:

I am a woman, a perfect creation of God's. I clean my outer body with soap; and my inner "body" with truth and a new tape. My inner cleanliness is determined by what is inside me, and I try to be clean of heart and mind. God looks at my inner beauty and judges me accordingly. When he finds an area of my life that is dirty, I will ask that he point it out to me. Then I can ask for forgiveness and about how to properly clean up that area so that I can feel cleaner with and about myself. I don't want to judge others by virtue of their sex, and I likewise don't accept their judgment via my sex. I don't want to vomit today, and I may not tomorrow.

Joanie is twenty-two and a newlywed.

Every time my husband touches me, I feel like something I can't identify is sucking the breath right out of my lungs. I feel boxed in a tight cage with nowhere to turn and no way to breathe. I'm panicky and afraid I'll suffocate. I've tried to just endure it, but that isn't fair to either one of us. What could it mean? I love my husband but I can't stand being with him. After sex I am relieved and feel like I've done a service, somehow performed, and received an "A," as if I'm free for awhile of an obligation, and I've done my "duty." I know it doesn't make any sense, and I've gone to doctors who tell me that physically I'm OK, and yet I dread going to bed at night. I don't feel Al is the reason for my trapped feeling, but nonetheless, we're both being short-changed. I can't wait for him to go to sleep at night so that I can release my own tension with food!

Thinking back, Joanie recalled her father holding her arms down and tickling her until it *hurt*. Also putting a pillow over her face until she thought she couldn't breathe anymore. She knew she was a very sexual woman, and felt punished because she couldn't allow the release that sexual gratification could bring. But the early taping of "Dad" and the forced "fun" made it impossible until she could actually "see" and feel the incident again. Lying with her husband brought back the same suffocation and paralyzing feeling. Every time she would start to remember, she would block the very accurate account by binging. She felt a definite, temporary gratification from the food, and it was enough to put off the remembrance again and again. It was too painful to think perhaps Dad was being cruel to her by such horseplay. But when she was able to recognize this real possibility, it was very much preferable to that of facing it by "proxy" with her husband every time he came near her.

Her dad's roughness was not good, but it was only representative of one area, one in his character. It did not mean that he was a bad father in every other area. Relief. She didn't have to judge him or hate him. Instead she was able to forgive him for doing it, forgive herself for not enjoying her husband, and hate instead, the incident itself. Forgive her father . . . love her husband . . . like herself . . . close the refrigerator . . . release!

All three women shared a common bond. Their tapes were playing negative but real accounts from the past which were continuing to be heard, believed, and perpetuated.

The assault on Ruth's sexual identity was an implied one, and therefore hard for her to "put her finger on" and identify. But it was an assault all the same. Joanie's and Sarah's were frontal attacks that seemed to scream, "You are guilty by virtue of your sex!" Sarah's tape indicated that being a girl was shameful, while Joanie's demanded that to be a female was to endure being overpowered, trapped, and forced to comply. To them, to be a woman was to be condemned without a trial, and it was its own punishment.

These women, and many more like them, feel their femininity has been judged and found guilty, literally by virtue of their sex. They carry out their own sentence every day by replaying the same verdict from the tapes, over and over. The damaging tapes were not perceived inaccurately; rather they were factual assaults on their femininity and their identities as young girls and future women. By no means were they figments of their imagination! But the past is done, and there is no reason why it should continue to rule the present or reflect the future. Let's acknowledge the truth—judge the tapes, and not other people or ourselves!

I'd like to cover one more area of womanhood that I have experienced. As a girl, my role model was my mother. Mom was always my best friend. She was, and remains today, a beautiful human being; our friendship continues to grow. As a girl, my mother represented all other mothers, wives, and women in general. I never knew another woman personally. I watched her "being a woman" in all areas of her life and judged my own femininity accordingly.

However, my own personality was and is very different from my mother's. I can see that now, but I didn't at the time. In my childishness I thought it was required that I emulate her role as I grew, and eventually copy it as an adult.

Like the chameleon, the little animal who changes its color, thus enabling it to fit into any threatening environment, I determined it was safer to change my "color" with each person or situation than to risk being my own person. As such I was not developing my own identity, or my own femininity. I was dependent on whomever I was around. I needed to go to college and find the profession that would best fit my personality and character traits, instead of trying to fit into a role, a profession that didn't fit me at all.

I married at nineteen because I thought marriage would validate my confused feelings about womanhood and help me feel more comfortable with myself and my identity. But it didn't; I felt like a second-hand citizen instead of a helpmate and nucleus of the family.

Next step? The fulfillment must come from motherhood. I had a baby, my joy and precious son, Jeff. I was now a wife and a mother, but I still felt invalidated as a woman.

Mom had been a happy homemaker who had worked outside the home only to help supplement the family income, not to fulfill a need to find her identity as a woman. Neither one of us realized that I needed to identify my own place as a woman, validate my own femininity. My role of wife and mother was and is important to me; but it is not the validation of my womanhood. I was trying to play a role that fit my mother, but not me.

I can feel just as much a woman by finding my own identity, my own happiness; but I won't get there by emulating my mother. I choose not to be a chameleon ... not to change my colors according to other people or their judgment. I feel every inch a woman by pursuing my own talents and brand of happiness—what works for me. I like to believe my reaching out enhances my role as wife and mother, rather than detracts from it. I am feminine when I feel good about my female identity, not when I am trying to adapt to someone else's view or identity.

As bulimic women, one alternative open to us is to try to relieve the incidents that could "traumatize" and influence our own children's tapes. We have a wonderful opportunity to help our kids understand our vulnerabilities and weaknesses, to see us just as people practicing parenthood, not as God almighty. We fall from the pedestal, and so can they. We're vulnerable, and so are they. We're not perfect, so they don't have to be either.

EIGHT
ALONE AGAIN

It was five years before I had shared my bulimia with my family. It had never occurred to me during those first years to let others into such a "weak" area of my life. I didn't even want to share it with myself!

My first reaction to my weakness in the past had been immediately to deny it and to shut myself off from everyone. It was such a well-rehearsed pattern of behavior, I wasn't even aware I was doing it.

I had always felt apart, separate somehow from everyone else in my life. This separateness was like a protection, a hope chest that I kept hidden under the bed. If I could forget about it, and no one else knew of the chest's existence, then I could survive. It was safer to isolate myself than to pull that chest out from under the bed. Exposure meant coming face to face with a weakness, a frailty I had long ago decided I was ashamed of, and a trait that was unacceptable because it would cause judgment to rain down upon me from heaven, from my family and peers, and from myself.

Sometimes I'd hear a little voice inside me saying, "I dare you to look inside and find out why you binge and purge. I dare you to discover why the bulimia and isolation are easier to accept than the weaknesses that permitted such character flaws in the first place." Oh, how I used to hate a dare! It seemed to indicate guts; something I felt I lacked. The opposite of guts was cowardice to me, and cowardice was definitely a reason to hide! It was one of the weaknesses I had carefully tucked away in my chest. I was afraid to find out why I shut myself off from other people, why I was afraid and a coward.

How could I beg, borrow, or steal the guts to dare to unlock, dare to look, dare to feel and then—dare to expose all my dirty weaknesses? Where could I find the guts to "dare to dare" in the first place? And what if I did dare to pull the chest out from under the bed? I'm scared to death to expose the contents in front of myself. What if someone else saw me looking in it? I'd be subject to public ridicule! I'm not ready to invite anyone in to look at it with me. I'd be judged weak and expected to change.

Suddenly I'd have to become a brave woman who dares to be herself no matter what. I'd have to go back to school and become the first woman president of the United States, or at least discover a cure for the common cold! *Hated if I don't,* and ostracized from my family and society at large! *Doomed if I do, doomed if I don't!* Oh, well. Maybe if I shove the chest a little farther under the bed so that I can't see it and be reminded of its "creepy" contents.

I tried so hard to keep my bulimia a secret because it seemed almost acceptable, as long as I was able to keep the reasons for it tucked safely away in the friendly hope chest of isolation. But just as the playpen became a cage, my hope chest was turning into my volcano.

If you've decided it's time to pull out that hope chest from under the bed, to dust it off and discover the reasons for the symptom of isolation, let me give you a hint. When the women I counsel are having difficulty pinpointing the "whys," I ask them to devote at least a week to searching their computer banks for a tape that will help them "take a walk down memory lane." Objective? The remembering of their earliest recollection. Many times a first memory is an unpleasant one; thus the isolation process begins as a protection.

It may take a little while to allow the tape to replay that first memory without your trying to block the pain out, or color its truth with a protection memory. It is hard for some to go back into an uncomfortable memory without making excuses for it, but hang in there!

Terri, a mother of two, recalled her mother handing her over to an orphanage at age four. The experience was always painful to remember, but more than that, it was traumatic to finally allow herself to see what really hurt: an absence of tears in her mother's eyes.

"Why didn't she cry; was she throwing me away?" Terri wanted to believe the half of the tape that indicated that Mom was unhappy with the situation; however, the other half that recorded that her mother didn't cry, had been blocked as a protection against even more pain. She didn't want to be able to remember that half, but she couldn't erase the tape. It played just often enough to make her uncomfortable.

At the orphanage, she isolated herself from the other children because she said she felt unworthy of their friendship, but didn't know why. The "other" half of the tape was subtly being heard. For the next fifteen years, she confusedly believed she was unworthy, without understanding why. This was true in all present and future relationships. By finally acknowledging the complete memory, she was able to experience the feeling of abandonment and the subsequent insecurity and shame of not being wanted. She questioned her mother, whose explanation was more than satisfactory: "I didn't want to make it any harder for you to leave me than it already was, so I held the tears in until I could get home. I cried so hard I couldn't eat or sleep for three days. I didn't know what else to do, there simply was no more money, and I wasn't able to feed you anymore."

Terri had not allowed herself to remember the abandonment as being anything but forced on her and her mother. Yet the fear of not being wanted by her mother was there, recorded on her tape, just not being permitted to penetrate and be recognized—hence the isolation.

I'll share my earliest memory, my first isolation. Once upon a time there was a little girl . . . and in many ways, she stayed there.

My first encounter with isolation was my earliest memory. It took place at age three. My mother, having just given birth to my brother Michael, was lying in a hospital bed, looking as white as the sheet that was clinging to her weakened body. I remember being sneaked into the room via an open window and told to be very quiet because I wasn't supposed to be there, and wondering why not. To a small girl, that room was huge, as if all the dividing partitions in the hospital had been removed and there was nothing but this big, empty ward.

There was only me, my grandmother, Dad, Mom, and this strange thing lying by her side. Everything was so largely out of proportion in the room, except for Mom, who was so small and frail. I was being prodded to get into the bed with her, but I didn't want to. She was sick. How could she have allowed that?

Something was terribly wrong, and this place was her punishment.

This isn't my mother; I don't know this fragile, weak person. If she is Mom, then she has somehow betrayed me by her fragility.

I was afraid for *me,* not her. If she could be this hurt, how could she take care of me anymore? I felt as though God was lying in that bed, sick and dying, and I was no longer safe. Mom had become part of a white and sterile web that was controlling and manipulating her into participating in my own capture as well as hers. I felt like a helpless and small bug caught in this web. Could I get sick like her? Could I catch the sickness and become as helpless as she was? How could Mom be so vulnerable? Were we both already captured? My fear took on a forbidding and threatening odor, and even today I identify that threatening smell of chloroform and alcohol with fear. I was cold, insecure, and confused. The chill enveloped me. I was frightened of the pervasive fear and rising doubts as to my safety.

As I continued to recall the experience, I could see that those doubts also included my shame. Shame, because all I wanted to do was run away from my mother, the one person I loved more than anything in the world. I wanted to run away as fast as possible, and emotionally, I did just that.

A week later when an ambulance brought Mom and Mike home from the hospital, I was thrilled to have her back again, and very excited about my new baby brother. I no longer chose to remember her as susceptible and sick. But I also didn't feel as safe anymore. I was fearful and there was an insecurity, a loneliness building that I didn't understand. I hid the feeling away as best I could, but I had begun pulling away . . . separating . . . isolating myself.

Remembering and identifying that first isolation memory can be a tremendous release, and it may help to encourage your computer to yield even more clues. Keep trying.

Another form of my isolation revolved around the television and weekends. My family were outdoor people and weekends meant planning activities that didn't take place in the house. Mom and Dad would work in the yard; Mike usually played war by the garage; and I was completely enthralled by the television. All alone, and about a foot away from the screen, I would watch all the old black and white movies, all day long if possible.

I'd hear the family call me to come outside and join them, but I'd pretend I didn't hear. I desperately wanted to become absorbed in the stories that unfolded every hour and a half, and gladly would have shrunk into the tube and become a part of the magical fantasies dancing in front of me, if I could have. There, within a seven-inch screen, was a wonderful acceptance and freedom I didn't permit myself. Even if no love was lost in the beginning frames of the movies, sooner or later, as the plot emerged, a beautiful and forgiving reconciliation took place, to everyone's mutual satisfaction. Oh, how I wished real life could be as forgiving. But it was better to live my fantasies through the tube; it was safer. Isolation.

I'm fourteen years old, and I'm scared! Scared to tell anyone and scared my family will think I'm a coward. I don't want to admit the awful truth. O dear God, how I fear the truth! I don't know why I'm so scared. What kind of answer is that? Who'll want to listen to me whine about some weakness I can't even describe!

Sometimes I fear going to sleep. I'm afraid even to go to bed! My brother and I share the same bedroom— you'd think I'd feel safe, not alone, but I don't. He doesn't know I'm in danger of my elusive fear, and I don't tell him. It's late and dark, and my brother, Mike, is asleep. Mom and Dad are also asleep in the next room. I'm especially terrified when my family turns their back on me by going to sleep, leaving me alone and so vulnerable to the consuming night.

It lasts so long! They sleep so hard! I wish I could wake Mom; but she works all day long, so I couldn't do that. Besides, it would wake Dad and he would tell me not to be silly, and to go back to bed. Oh, I wish I could crawl in bed with Mom. If I woke Mike he might get scared, too, and I wouldn't want that—he's younger and I feel responsible for him. He has terrible leg aches—growing pains, the doctor calls them, and I rub them at night before he goes to sleep. I enjoy taking care of him and being the one he turns to at night. I don't want to destroy or jeopardize his confidence in me.

Everyone is sound asleep and I'm sitting up in bed with my back to the wall, being just as quiet as possible—waiting. I watch the shadows fall across the floor, wondering which one will be the one that kills me. I imagine that every creak the house makes is the front door opening to my fear. I'm alone—and I can't let anyone in on my aloneness; the family wouldn't understand. They would think I was silly. Isolation.

When I do fall asleep, I have a recurring dream. I'm in the clouds with my dad—there is a general store there and I am holding Dad's hand as he talks to the other men in the store. I am very small, and it feels secure to have my hand in his. I hear a noise and turn to see a huge steamroller approaching the store. I don't know how, but I am aware it is coming to run over me alone. The noise is deafening and I turn to my dad to see his reaction, to see if my fear is legitimate. But he doesn't hear me, nor does he seem aware of the impending danger as he continues to talk to his friends, ignoring me. I start to scream, and he drops my hand. He seems too busy talking even to notice. I become frantic in my fear, but am unable to move. I'm right there, standing beside my dad, screaming at the top of my lungs, but it's no use. I'm alone—I'm about to die and no one will help me. It doesn't do any good to call out. Isolation.

I'm fifteen. My only friend is sick and staying home from school today; she could go if she really wanted to! Why is she forcing me to go to school alone. I'm walking down the hall corridors. Everywhere kids are calling to one another, laughing, and I'm sweating again. I'm terrified they'll notice I'm alone, terrified no one will want to talk to me, be with me. Why don't I ever fit? I can't tell anyone, they'd think I was crazy. In the classroom everyone seems to be listening to the teacher. I'm watching them, afraid they'll notice me, afraid they'll ignore me. What if the teacher calls on me? I won't know the answer; everyone will know how stupid I am. Hurry clock, tick away the fear—let me go home where I can hide. If only I could tell Mom or Dad. But they're tired. They both have legitimate jobs, and legitimate reasons to be tired. My stupid fears aren't worth their attention. Besides, I still believe they would judge me a weak coward for such foolishness. I have to keep my fear to myself and learn once and for all to be separate from everyone else. Isolation.

I'm a mother with a newborn baby. I've never babysat in my life, or changed a baby, or even held a baby. Suddenly, I don't feel very good, and this thing won't shut up. Where is my mothering instinct? Am I crazy? Why don't I love this creation of my husband and me? It's a stranger that has intruded into my life, and I can't go anywhere I want or do what I want. What am I going to do? I don't dare tell anyone else. What would people think? I'm sure all other mothers are ecstatic with their new offspring. My mom works all the time, and I can't expect her to take him off my hands. Everyone will think I'm a terrible person. So I keep it to myself. Isolation.

Twenty-two and a "brand new Christian." I've accepted Jesus Christ as my Savior and I'm going to heaven! I can't wait to tell everyone. Only when I do, they're not excited. I feel silly, as if I were trying to explain the theory of relativity. I barely understand what's happened myself, and the Bible might as well be written in Greek! When I share my experience with my husband, he rolls his eyes around in his head, as if to say, "Here we go again." And if I mention it to anyone else, he looks at me as if I were a small child who still thinks Santa Claus lives at the North Pole.

Where do I go to be with others of my own kind—a church? I feel funny by myself. A Bible study? They all seem to know one another already. I realize I should give it time, but I don't feel like I'll ever fit. They seem holier, cleaner than me—somehow. I'm uncomfortable. I'm "in school" again, alone again, not "fitting in" again—what should I do? I won't talk about my faith with anyone and I won't try to convince church people of their need to include me. I'll pull away; it's safer that way. I'm not happy, but the pressure of having to fit in will ease and I can crawl back into my shell again. Isolation.

NINE
FEELING THE
BLUES

I look at others and see technicolor dancers rhythmically swirling to a fast beat. I look in the mirror and see a black and white wallflower tripping over her own feet . . . that's depressing. All the others seem to gather confidence through life by tightening the laces on their track shoes to insure a race to the finish. But I'm encumbered as usual with cement galoshes—forever trying to find my own confidence, the elusive starting line. That's depressing and frustrating.

To me, though, depression was more than just feelings of inadequacy and unhappiness. It was feeling like I was in a coma with my eyes staring wide open, somehow continuing to perform for everyone around me, while inside feeling like a rotting vegetable, with nothing left for my intellect to gnaw on but numb despair and hopelessness. Even so, I would still manage to worry about what the neighbors would think if I let the garbage cans sit out overnight. That went beyond *depressing,* and into *a depression.* . . .

That's what it felt like, but what is it? The dictionary says depression is a decrease in force or activity.

Boy, could I ever relate to that! When depressed, I was aware only of not trying or caring if I were anywhere else. When in that seemingly stagnate state, I temporarily gave up; nothing seemed to matter, and yet it was never enough to stop my needing the approval of other people, or to stop performing for them.

A depression was like a toothache; somehow I had to get to the "root" of the pain, to touch the "nerve" that led to "insatiable" hopelessness, to identify it, and to "fill" it with more understanding and growth.

I often say that bulimia is a depression I had all of my life, so to continue to fall prey to its entrapment was never going to get me anywhere with the other symptoms. I was going to have to face the dirty thing during one of the attacks, and deal with it as best I could.

If I could go back and tap my memory tapes for relief from the symptom of isolation, then I could do the same with depression, which seemed to both accompany and follow isolation. Then I could tackle the more current symptoms of binging and purging.

If to be depressed is to temporarily give up to an identifiable despair, there had to be an original and very tangible parent feeling of despair and hopelessness. Back to the dictionary: *depressor*: something that slowly draws down a part of the body (such as my befoggled brain). Now I'm getting somewhere! The depressor had to be my "tapes," which were, without a single thought to my sanity, periodically replaying the original memory, the original incident or incidents of despair. With my usual aplomb, I was again blocking their source and identity. The only distinguishable sounds which sifted through to me were those somehow associated with the *now* and the despair. In other words, a sound, a location, a time of day, or a parallel situation would trigger the original memory, and the tape would play again, never completely penetrating the complete facts.

It would have scared me if I thought I were going to have to go through it alone. However, I believed in God, and I knew he would never leave me. I believed he would go through it with me. Armed with my faith, I took Mr. Webster's definition of a depressor also as a promise from my Heavenly Father. "If I am a part of God's family, nothing can draw me down without his permission and acknowledgment. So, depression must be a way that God communicates in order to help me better understand myself."

To me, that indicates that it was not only possible, but probable that I could survive a depression with him as my guide. I could learn how to better cope with my illness, how to better understand myself—now and in the future. These negative and condemning tapes, the haunting memories, were demanding that I react as negatively to *now* situations as I did to those in the past.

I'm not talking about recovering from a death, losing a job, or going through a divorce, but rather a depression that you can't seem to identify, which attacks like an old and faithful enemy. My depressions were plugged into the past—my inability to sort out inadequacies and fears. Thus the tape would keep assuring me I couldn't handle them now. Depression.

My first stab at understanding was very time consuming. I sat in my living room and closed my eyes. *What am I supposed to be trying to do?* I wasn't sure, but I did know that this particular depression seemed always to take place in the afternoon. Why? Sometimes I would be thinking about something else, even be happy, then boom—depression: an overwhelming desire to let the world go by without lifting a finger to become a part of it, to emotionally tune out for the duration.

Think ... nothing ... think ... a black cloud, a thick gray blanket of forgetfulness, a paralyzing fog with a way out ... nothing ..."

It took days for the fog to lift, but when it did, I saw a small girl looking out a plate glass window, terrified of what was in the house with her. Outside was clean and free, but she felt compelled to stay inside and wait. Soon other members of the family would come home, but for now ... there was only her—and the fear. Always the fear of the unknown, the elusive stranger who would make her life such a living hell, terrified even to turn around, or to make a sound. I felt once more the terror that little girl felt.

But what was the identity of the stranger, the devil who haunted me, and me alone? As I continued to live the pattern of fear over again, suddenly the stranger had a name. It was as if he wore a sign around his neck. Turning, I read the sign and couldn't believe my eyes. Like a neon light it came on— *loneliness.* All my life I had been terrified of this person, this thing. As a child I didn't have the insight to recognize my real enemy, my separateness, my isolation, and my depression. My isolation was a defense, but it had only created loneliness and depression. When I opened my eyes, I was crying for that little girl, but I was relieved and delighted. It broke the afternoon "blahs," and I had my insight. You see, afternoons were always a danger time for me. There was always the temptation to go on a binge. So to go through one of the cycles without following into a depression was pure bliss.

I knew I wasn't ready to "fix it" that day, but I was so grateful for the opportunity just to identify it and look at it honestly. I'd fix it when I had given myself time to absorb its reality, and to confide in God.

I knew I had found a key to future depressions. When "it" happened again, I could sit down and wait for the fog to lift, and experience the tape as it occurred without blocking it.

I got my second chance the latter part of the same week. Just outside my office window is a lovely maple tree; lovely—and depressing. Every time I admired its beautiful leaves, I went into a fog of withdrawal that just had to wear off rather than be understood. Again, I sat down, looked at the tree, experienced the fog, and closed my eyes. The gray blanket fell over my brain, trying to make me block the memory. I waited . . . then the clearing, and the remembrance.

My office becomes Jeff's bedroom, and he is a baby in his crib. I am looking out the window at a smaller version of that same tree, feeling helpless and desolate. I am trapped, forced to stay inside and take care of my baby. The world is going on outside my window. People are creating new lives. They're having fun with other people, laughing and creating memories . . . living!

My husband worked fifteen hours a day when Jeff was first born, only seeing us at night around midnight. It seemed the world existed for everyone else, but was standing still for me. I didn't matter. My youth was passing me by. I knew I was being selfish. Ron worked hard all day and didn't like being away. I knew many women were in the same boat, so I kept my despair to myself, thinking that to admit the feelings would show the world what a terrible, selfish, worthless woman I really was. My feelings were never legitimate. After all, I was only a housewife doing nothing all day.

I needed to connect my depression with the experience from the past, to replay the tape that I had been blocking because it might be painful or because I felt it was foolish. By realizing what the tree had come to mean to me as the years passed, I was able to say to my computer: "The past is done. I am no longer that trapped woman with nowhere to go with my despair. The tree is beautiful, and I use my office to help free myself now and in the future through my writing. The entrapment of motherhood did not last long, and was not my bondage alone. Many experience post-baby blues. It does not indicate that I was a bad mother. I loved my son then, and love him now. I can experience negative feelings without harboring shame and guilt for the rest of my life. It's time to put that behind me and get on with the present." I never suffered that depression again.

In Isaiah 42:7, the Bible says, "You will open the eyes of the blind and release those who sit in prison darkness and despair." I had to dare to take the blinders off, and dare to go through the depressions with God by my side.

TEN
DON'T FENCE
ME IN

I don't know what control means to you, but I now know what it meant to me! I was thrashing around like a chicken with my head cut off in a desperate frenzy to do as much as possible, for as many as possible, in as short a time as possible—and all for the privilege of being able to crawl back into my self-made hole of isolation so I could observe the big, bad world. When I was isolated, I felt safe. Believe me, that wasn't an easy accomplishment. Hiding is an art in itself, and that's exactly what I was doing in my camouflage bid to be all things to all people—constantly scrambling to please everyone enough to be accepted or at least to go partially unnoticed. It is an exhausting and scary business, a very emotionally precarious way to exist and, at the same time, to hide.

You see, I really was not the shy little girl with neat pigtails. No, indeed. Inside where the "I" *really* lived, hid a very angry, fat, big, and clumsy infant that would have preferred everyone's evaporation rather than have them share her carefully guarded lack of identity. I had to be forever thinking of new ways to be accepted. Or at least of the next best thing, just to be left alone. I had to keep the elusive "them" from discovering that I wasn't really fitting in at all. I was only masquerading as an equal, all the while dying inside and scared to death that they would unmask "Jackie the fraud"—leaving me as lonely on the outside as I felt on the inside. Does this make sense? That's all right; it didn't to me at the time, either.

If it sounds like I was a quivering bowl of jelly with no mind of my own, that's because it's how I felt inside—all the time. Why didn't I reach out for help? What good did it do me to try to keep my depression a deep, dark secret for so many years? No one could have thought any less of me than *I* already did. The problem was, I didn't know the deep, dark secret even existed! What I was conscious of was an awesome fear that every now and then would work its way to the surface in its bid to be identified. Now I know that secret was my inability to develop an identity of my own. I feared "it" would threaten me by revealing "itself" to others. This "betrayal feeling" was imminent whenever I failed to successfully fit in. When that happened, my immediate reaction was to fall back and retreat into my faithful companion and symptom—isolation. Isolated, I still felt the threat of the world catching me and thus exposing the secret. But at least I felt temporarily safe again.

There was a song my parents used to sing when I was a girl that kept running through my mind at the most unusual times. I could not then, or now, tell you how the song goes, nor could I "hum a few bars" but somehow I could relate to the title—"Don't Fence Me In." It always struck a chord in my memory, a reminder of that unexplained unhappiness and anger.

It shouted at me when I remembered the class election speeches back in grade school. An assembly was called, and I was looking forward to mingling unnoticed on the lawn, listening and watching attentively as all of the popular kids would begin filing in front of me. I loved observing from afar the perfect role models on parade. (I got the same kick from watching soap operas much later on.) Every election was a fashion show and popularity contest. Whoever was the most popular kid in school was awarded the class presidency, etc. These were the cream of the crop, out to reassert and protect their crowns. Preceding each entrance was an advance man—the layer of red carpet, the campaign manager.

The big day brought each candidate in his or her Sunday best, all set to perform—to be adored by the waiting public, the audience. Eagerly looking forward to the show and feeling very safe in wondering how anyone could possibly have that much nerve, I left my first class and literally ran into Cynthia, "the drip." I had never cared for her. She had the personality of a slug, and I was afraid it might somehow rub off. She had this annoying habit of thinking (out loud, no less), that she was just as good as everyone else in school. I never bothered to correct her. Come to think of it, I never bothered to speak to her, because her ideas were too ludicrous to discuss. Her clothes were off the rack; she was unattractive, and she didn't seem all that bright.

Kids like us simply did not confuse our stations in life with that of the elite. I despised her because she didn't realize she was out of it. She never played by the rules, mine anyway, and was a constant reminder of what I would look like if I ever dared to break my rule of anonymity. Here she was, directly in my path, and apparently on purpose.

Deliberately seeking me out, she proceeded to mortify me with the most ridiculous proposition I had ever heard. She was actually going to run for a class position, and she wanted me to be her campaign manager! She was disheveled. It was an hour before the big event, and she had already asked everyone else in the school. Of course, she had been refused! She was a loser, the most unpopular girl in the school! Of all the unmitigated gall! I would rather have been dragged through the assembly stark naked (well, almost) than to appear in such company and be laughed off the campus for sheer stupidity!

"Are you so unconscious you aren't aware that this whole thing is a popularity contest, a command performance that the rest of us are only barely allowed to watch from a distance? I won't even go into the insult of your informing me that I'm your last hope, nor that you've actually had the guts to share it with me! Two losers on the same platform? Get away from me!"

The louder and more threatened I became, the more panicky and adamant she became.

"Please, I'm as good as anyone else here. I could do the job, and I deserve a chance like everybody else. But if you won't be my campaign manager, I'll be denied that chance. All I'm asking you to do is stand up there for one minute and introduce me—not sing my praises, just introduce me. Is that asking too much?"

You bet it was! But I was trapped. I couldn't believe my ears, her nerve, or my eventual response: Yes.

What had I done? I'd be exposed in front of the entire student body. And for Cynthia, the "twit"! My name would be associated with hers forever. Why had I consented? How could I be forced into betraying myself like this? Never, never, had I agreed to such a stupid thing in my whole life. Maybe "they" wouldn't even be listening; after all, no one knew her name or mine. Perhaps we'd go unnoticed, quickly on and just as quickly off.

We waited our turn into the lions den, all the while

I was dying with each tick of the clock.

"And now, campaign manager for Cynthia (the twit) is Jackie McLendon." Silence. Deafening and overwhelmingly judgmental silence. I had thought surely someone would at least rub his hands together briefly, if for no other reason than to signal getting on with it. But no, nothing. I said my dumb one-minute intro, then all but ran from the podium. Cynthia emerged to a few chuckles, then launched into a ten-minute oratory on her oblique qualifications, none of which included whom she knew or what football player she dated. Afterward, she didn't even thank me!

Needless to say, Cynthia won nothing . . . that day, anyway. Me? I made up my mind never again to expose a feeling that was capable of hurting me, and that included the occasional humanitarian sense of decency and fair play. Let the stronger save the world; let *them* do someone a favor. I didn't care if the underdog did have a say coming, let him say it on his own. It seemed as if all exposed emotion was painful. Enough. I'd go back to just fitting in and be content. That is contentment, isn't it?

Believe it or not, I wondered whatever became of Cynthia several times while I was consuming the refrigerator. She probably went on to be a congresswoman. I went on with my binge.

I heard the confusing song title again when I dumped my very best childhood friend because she threatened my desired identity. I wanted to become a stronger person, but the only way I knew how to do that was to latch on to a stronger friend.

When it was terribly current to read *Time* magazine and discuss the starving children of India, she was interested in cruising and boys. There was absolutely nothing wrong in the direction she was going, except—I didn't have the strength of my own identity to allow her to be herself, and me to be myself. Being friends with Lila didn't fit into the new image I was trying to project upon myself. I would have to find someone who balanced me better so I could once again latch on and fit. I simply did not know how to be my own person and still be her friend. I was afraid of becoming her, but I didn't know how to tell her. I didn't understand how terrified I was of being absorbed into her pattern and becoming lost forever.

So in order to escape from the unknown fear, I avoided her altogether. I made sure I wasn't home when she came over, and never answered the phone. I completely disregarded her feelings, and ignored her existence. I hated myself for treating her so shabbily, but rationalized that she was better off without me. I just wanted to run away and never come back! Everyone was either a threat or a way out, as I changed my colors in a bid to fit and hide, or escape and hide. I didn't know how to be my own person. And that particular time, Lila paid the price.

One time I finally talked my dad into letting me have a piano and take lessons, only to quit because I felt the pressure of having to perform, show, or prove to others what I had thus learned or hadn't learned. There was no doubt in my mind that my father could have been a concert pianist with the same amount of lessons; so rather than perform and risk his "supposed" anger and disappointment, I stopped practicing altogether. I stopped trying. Dad sold the piano, and I imagined him thinking, "I knew she wouldn't stay with it; it was a waste of money and time." It was painful to give up the lessons and the dream of playing well. I even enjoyed the practice. But even more painful was the risk of having to perform for others who would happen to drop by on occasion, or the fear that I would fail Dad by hitting the inevitable wrong notes.

He wouldn't have cared as long as I had dared to try, and was always telling me so. But, in my own insecurity, all I heard was, "You'll only fail again, and this time I will not forgive you or give you a second chance." I wanted the piano to be mine and mine alone, my comforter and my friend. But how do you take a piano to your room and announce, "I want to be alone!" I wanted to play for myself. I didn't mind if I hit "klunkers." But performing meant perfection, so I refused to try.

Why? Why did these fragmented memories connect somehow with a song title? I stopped the tape one afternoon recently as it was playing. I had just broken another tennis date with three other women who had really been counting on me to complete a fourth. I felt crummy about reneging again and hated the subsequent lie. But I just couldn't seem to keep the commitment. I decided to search my memory banks once more for the answers. It had worked during my depression, and I was having flashbacks anyway. So, closing my eyes, I allowed the fog to lift and tried to connect the song title with an original memory from the past that would relate to the already strange recollection.

Nothing. I had to ask myself several questions to get rolling. What did the words "fence in" mean to me? It wasn't easy to concentrate. Impatience is very much a symptom of bulimia, and patience is very much a part of recovery. I asked for God's help, and let my mind search for the revealing tape that would bring enlightenment.

More sitting, more waiting, and the fog lifting. "Fence-in" indicated *control!* Even the word brought beads of perspiration to my already frowning brow. But why?

Recalling again that fitting seemed the safest way to be accepted and then left alone, what was that saying about my sense of freedom, my space to be myself? Instead of safety, I was giving permission for everyone else to control my feelings and determine how I was to react. I never initiated anything, I always reacted to what happened. By allowing this control, I felt controlled and forced to comply. But I didn't know what to do about it and how to manage to fit in. In insisting that everyone else set the tempo for my moods, I had to become a very good actress.

For example, if upon arising for the day, I was conscious of being depressed, I had to switch gears and adapt to the mood of the person I was about to be with. That is not always an easy thing to do. Hiding emotional pain is difficult, but necessary if one is endeavoring to fit in. I first had to be noncommittal in order to determine the other person's mood, then switch gears and convince him of my sincerity.

Now, back to the chameleon. Dad's personality was so powerful that for me to fit in meant faking or becoming meek. Two bulls in the same arena just don't mix. That way I was less apt to offend, less apt to upset him, and less apt to have to initiate rather than respond. He was a leader; I followed.

When in school I had tried to stay in the background as much as possible, all the while really wanting to assert myself and become one of "them," but always afraid. I definitely did not make waves for fear of being washed ashore! But in doing so, I was merely avoiding my real personality, ignoring the traits that would have enabled me to continue growing emotionally as well as physically. I was like my father in many ways, but I thought two of him could not have survived in the same house.

Don't fence me in? Who? It was I doing the fencing in. I was screaming, *Don't allow others to determine your reactions! Don't give them permission to control your feelings, and then force yourself to comply with that control! Break through the fence and dare to walk in the freedom of being yourself!* There was a part of me that was screaming about freedom, but in my fright and lack of understanding, I couldn't and wouldn't listen for fear of hearing and hating the risk involved.

Here's an example of my catching other people's moods—one I could live with. I'll never forget my high school bookkeeping class. Every day we would stand outside and wait for the teacher to unlock the classroom door. Friends always grouped together as usual, and I stood as usual with my one safe pal. One girl in particular perpetually caught my eye because she had the most pleasant and constant smile I had ever seen. I looked forward to her pleasing face every day. As she was signing my yearbook on the last day of school, I was dumbfounded to read what she had quickly written. *To Jackie: I have never known anyone who always smiled, no matter what was happening in her life. I don't know how you do it, but I wish I could do the same, for it is a real inspiration to me.* Seeing her smile was absolutely the only time I ever dared to show any emotion at all. I couldn't help but emulate her pleasantness—it was marvelously catching! I wish it had been all good traits I copied from other people.

Copying others' personalities in order to fit in is never good. Only to react, as a means of being accepted, is never good. I needed to disagree with my dad and my peers. I needed to risk the terrible "what ifs." I needed to see that to disagree didn't mean immediate dismissal from the human race, only a difference of opinion. I needed to initiate responses from others for a change, to dare to put my foot in my mouth a few times in order to learn what not to do the next time. I needed to learn to grow in tact, but grow even if at times it meant being tactless. I needed to learn that sometimes even diplomacy isn't enough if someone is trying to manipulate or control in a manner that would be detrimental to my development.

Yes, my exposure through the campaign manager caper was painful, but I wish I had known or felt strong enough to see that you first have to crawl before you can walk. To shrink back didn't accomplish what it should have—growth through trial. I told no one about the incident; if I had, I know my dad would have said, "At least you dared to do something you felt was right. The only mistake you made was in accepting and absorbing the judgment of the others."

One thing I've learned through all of this is that it's never too late for me to make mistakes, to learn from them, to grow, and to be myself!

Much anger is associated with constantly asking others to tell you what mood you're in or what you're feeling. Not anger with the people initiating my reactions, but anger at myself for allowing such control over my life in the first place. It's a huge responsibility to ask or demand that others assume such control over your life.

For the first five years of binging and purging, and prior to my recognition of my symptoms, I didn't realize this anger existed. I was still too heavily into isolation, depression, and avoidance of all feelings, good or bad.

As time and my pattern of avoidance continued, indeed gathered momentum, the only area of responsibility I did choose to assume was for my weight. The years rolled on, and life became even harder to avoid or accept. Why did I settle on weight control as my only responsibility?

ELEVEN
WHY?

I must have asked myself that question a million times. Prior to my first all-out binge, overeating and dieting had somehow become synonymous. I reasoned that so many people were in the same boat, it must be normal. In truth, fitting in had simply become too much trouble. It was time to give it up for an easier form of safety control—weight. If I could only lose twenty-five pounds, then twenty. Finally ten pounds seemed to be all that separated me from true happiness. A hysterectomy and eight days of hospital stay enabled the loss, but alas, my happiness was short-lived. Along with recovery and a thinner me came uncharacteristic rages, crying jags, tremendous depressions, and eventually my old nemesis, the ten pounds returned. I tried hard to blame my behavior on an untimely menopause (I was in my early thirties), but in retrospect I think the operation was only the final straw that was to break the camel's back. Surgery had only been the trigger for the eruption of my already tremulous emotional volcano. Since childhood this volcano had been waiting, all the while building pressure that would lead to its inevitable explosion.

At this point I wasn't capable of understanding or coping with the confusing mood changes and rising inner turmoil, but I was very aware of a constant unhappiness and inability to feel good about myself. Something was tearing me apart! I was never content; rather I was calm one minute and furious the next. But over what? If I could only lose weight again, maybe everything would automatically fall into place.

Before, I had been able to cap the volcano by being very active in sports, especially tennis. I would play for two or three hours a day, clobbering the ball until I was exhausted—too exhausted to think. I tried hard to concentrate on ways to become a winner on the courts, taking countless lessons to insure my success. Practice and determination did bring a lot of pats on the back, a five-pound weight loss, and definitely a sense of pride. But no self-worth.

I was still five pounds too heavy, and now there were niggling little doubts to be dealt with: such as how valid it is to play half a day—every day—instead of devoting all my days to being the little woman. Plagued constantly, I continued to drag those nasty little doubts and my guilts to the courts.

After my surgical recovery was almost complete, I was feeling physically capable of returning to tennis again, but it no longer had the same pacifying effect on me. I couldn't keep my mind busy with thoughts of being just a tennis winner. Losing was devastating. I knew it was wrong to continue asking a sport to give me esteem, only to feel a loser when it came to self-worth. I couldn't become physically tired enough to settle my turmoil anymore. This turmoil was like a pointing finger that would jab me at the drop of a hat, or a decision! More and more, the pointing finger was becoming a tightening fist that was refusing to relax. I sensed a prevailing chill in the form of a premonition warning of a very hot and full volcano. It was getting ready to explode and erupt, once and for all, ready or not—but what if the eruption never stopped?

Frustration prevailed, and along with it the realization that I wasn't equipped to cap off anymore. The role of "Miss Suzie Homemaker," or the fantasy stand-in for Chris Evert-Lloyd no longer worked, and I wondered what would? In a "fix-it quick" frame of mind, I focused on an elusive, but familiar, cap for the volcano.

A total commitment to weight control would solve everything. Every meal would be regulated, discipline would become automatic, and I would truly be in *control* of each day. When those dirty suspicions about my marriage arose, I didn't eat for two days. If I felt like a parasite because I wasn't contributing to our income, I exercised more. It was constructive and quick!

My mind was being forced to conform to a brain-washing, just as my body was forced to respond to excessive exercise. To feel hunger was to succeed, and the less I ate, the less my mind could concentrate on the foul feelings. It was too busy justifying the refusal of the next meal.

I hoped I would begin losing those old doubts about my insecure future. Everyone knows that a thin person is not only sought after, but acceptable and very employable. When I became thin enough, there would be plenty of time to worry about the future anyway. No problem; my happiness through weight control would be ensured. Discipline equaled control, and weakness equaled hunger. To lose weight became my sole goal, my obsession and safety zone. The pounds came off and I felt a power I had experienced before as a teenager. Refusing to eat had enabled a sense of freedom and control.

Now there was a sense of future accomplishment

and self-worth. At last I was worthy! At last I was controlled. The accomplishment came from losing the weight, the esteem from being very thin and therefore a controlled person, and the self-worth from training my mind to deprive itself of food and thus not giving in to the primal urges of hunger. Gone was the nagging limp puppet feelings of always being at the mercy of anyone who chose to pull my strings—including the insecure and hungry me. Now the perpetual spasms of doubt and inadequacy were going away. Weren't they?

Finally, I was a winner! If I could *control* nothing else in my life, I could *control* my weight. The thinner I became, the more powerful I felt. Even the frightening rages and depressions didn't seem as bothersome. All my self-esteem and worth were being derived solely from the distortion of my body's image, and my mind's entrapment—more and more emphasis was able to be placed on being thin.

I assured myself that my control was composed of a permanent strength that could be held together by sheer will and determination. It was a hard and uncompromising strength I was able to rely on to protect me from facing fears and threatening emotions, and the cruel outside world.

However, its deceptive and inflexible dictatorship began to wear thinner and thinner. I was getting so weary of having to toe the line and constantly measure up to my dictating and unforgiving control. It demanded more and more allegiance, but eventually gave less and less protection. Food was a constant threat and so were the volcanic feelings. More and more the whys were plaguing me.

I can testify to the difficulty of coming up with answers for the emotional symptoms of bulimia. If these questions haven't as yet been faced, it's eventually impossible to understand them. *All right, now*

I'm thin—but what am I going to do with the rest of my life? I'm thin, but what if I can't get a good job because I don't have a formal education? I'm thin, but what if it's no guarantee I won't always be very, very frightened?

These uncomfortable "what ifs" were only the more immediate perplexities being avoided. Needless to say, I wasn't ready for the more complex questions, such as, why did I decide to not consciously feel or expose my emotions in the first place? Why was anger a dirty feeling; rejection a humiliation; loneliness indicative of a lack of pride; and boredom equivalent to laziness? Why weren't they considered legitimate feelings that could have helped me grow and blossom instead of withdraw and vegetate? Twinges of these unnerving awarenesses insisted on surfacing even as I kept trying to deceive myself into believing the same old lie. The deception continued to wear still thinner, and thinner—along with my body.

As a last effort to protect and preserve my deflating control through the obsession with overweight, I slid a little deeper into my world of pain and numbness. I carried a journal everywhere I went and recorded every calorie ingested. This was just the impetus needed to reassert my awesome control. Weight, food, calories. They were the enemy and as such underwent the intense scrutiny of my own private justification scales. They were allowed to stay only as long as my body could burn them up by the end of each day and thus rid itself of the dreaded cancer forever. I found that while I couldn't justify playing tennis for my enjoyment alone, I could justify excessive exercise whose objective was to help me become thin.

I joined a gym, going every other day, and in between showing my weary body no mercy. If I talked on the phone, which was clearly a waste of time, I jogged in place. If I listened to music or watched TV, another waste of time, more jogging to the music or floor exercises during commercials. There had to be a physical explanation for every movement, or a mental accounting for every action.

I remember hurting my back due to the strenuousness placed upon a very weak frame. Taking time out to go to my chiropractor really bothered me, and the fear of not being able to continue the obsessiveness chilled my blood. But the pain and fear of damage already done drove me to his office. The doctor left the room to allow a hot oil treatment to enhance the manipulation therapy. Feeling my control slipping even as I lay there, I forced myself to do leg exercises, even though it hurt. I had to know I was still able to control my body.

Every activity was designed to burn calories. At night I would scrutinize my journal to make sure fat hadn't somehow sneaked in and threatened my safety. I made a game of finding ways to eliminate even more of the obnoxious and esteem-destroying food. Hour after hour I devoured every new magazine article on exercise and weight control. I wanted desperately to emulate the beautiful models in the pictures who appeared so together, so happy, so perfect, so thin. I fantasized living their lives—another role I wished I could assume. They were perpetually free, in control, and thin.

If only I could lose another ten pounds. I was always trying to feel the same sense of accomplishment from the loss of each pound, as before, but in fact, I was feeling more confused and unhappy. Five more pounds came off; surely now the joy would come back and my measure of accomplishment would remain intact—only it didn't. The strain of pursuing perfection was showing more and more, mentally and physically. Horror of horrors ... no doubt about it ... I was hungry!

Oh, please, God! Tell me I have to carry a necklace of garlic around my neck and ward off attacks from blood-sucking vampires; or tell me I'm going to be in a life-and-death situation that threatens years of pain and suffering—but don't allow me to be hungry and unable to control the insufferable feeling I've fought so hard and so long to ignore and eliminate. I'm scared, not ready, and definitely not strong enough for such honesty. I can't face it. I don't want to hear about it. Or feel it!

Having vented my tantrum, I was ready for compromise. I'd eat a little more, but less often. I would allow myself a few of the no-nos that had been considered forbidden fruit. A little cake now and then, or a few cookies, and how about a donut—or two or three (they're small). This can be like Christmas— once in a while I'll open a present and it will satisfy me. After all, how long can I be expected to exist on 700 calories a day!

It was a time of firsts. To be experimenting with different foods and trying to loosen the long-sought-after and gained control. Food had either been safe or reserved for a binge. I didn't know how much to eat, nor how often. The opening of one package turned into a free-for-all—opening all the goodies, plus the Christmas tree, ornaments and all! Another phase of my bulimia, and binging had begun.

I thought my indiscretion was a fluke that would never, never happen again. But in truth it marked the beginning of a nightmare world of gorging. It was to be six months before the next indiscretion. Then four weeks. Then one week. Then every other day. Gorge—panic! Then came the other half of the cycle—the purge.

After a binge, the purging would guarantee the loss of weight added during the gorging. In between I ate nothing that could cause me to gain weight. My days were still ruled by my lack of food intake, and the related rituals. A normal day's menu would consist of: one slice of dry wheat toast in the morning, a three-ounce can of tuna on an enormous bed of lettuce for lunch, an apple and a dry baked potato for dinner. Ritualistically, the toast would be divided into exactly six bites, the lettuce for the tuna salad would be chopped for ten full minutes (very carefully so that every particle of tuna had touched and mingled with the lettuce), and the baked potato had to be eaten cold so that it would not taste too good (and thus encourage my ever wayward appetite). It was hard for me to think clearly when I wasn't eating enough food to enable me to think rationally. Naturally, helpful comments such as, "Pull yourself together and do something about this predicament," didn't do much good. My only reaction? "You just don't understand."

After five years of practicing and refining the art of binging and purging had passed and I had finally reached my ultimate bulimic accomplishment—I weighed ninety-five pounds. But the magical black numbers registering on the scales did not bring with them an expected heaven on earth. I had only two frustrations: being thin did not provide a permanent shelter in which to hide from the napping but not always sleeping volcano. And, secondly, how could I live with the pressure from staying on the ninety-five pound pedestal?

Can I binge less and purge more to stay there? If a pound would truly blow my cover and expose the horrible me to the world, then the scales become "Big Brother," and apply the screws to me by registering another pound. Talk about stress! As a safety device, my thinness was transient at best.

Each day brought the same threat. Did I gain an ounce and thus lose a measure of precious worth? That meant I was suddenly in jeopardy of losing the acceptance and approval I expected to be forthcoming from society and loved ones. And finally, why weren't they as impressed with my controlled thinness as I was? I had little patience for the comments of concerned family and friends who kept comparing my thin frame with that of starving concentration camp victims. Instead of adulation and flowers for my willpower, there were criticism and care packages.

As the end of my marathon years of feast or famine were drawing to a dismal conclusion, the horror of the cycles was occurring even more often. My panicky confusion was adding more fuel to my already full volcano. What I had set out to control, as a means of fixing everything wrong in my life, was now controlling me. I could not fast long enough in between each binge to compensate for the weight gain; and purging was scaring me. While one laxative would have been effective before, now it took many more, and I was told they were habit forming. Whereas vomiting was a last resort effort to rid myself of unwanted calories, I was soon compelled to exercise its temporary relief to keep down my rising inner turmoil. *What have I done to myself, and how can I stop it?*

Needless to say, I was also under a lot of guilt as I was lying to my family. When it became obvious to me "what" was controlling "who," I turned to the nearest person in my life, my husband, Ron. I told him about the binging. (I couldn't as yet expose the purging.) My gentle and kind husband registered shock, disbelief, and helplessness, but only until he could suggest some answers. He began marching me off to doctors in an effort to discover why I kept losing weight if I was binging. My coloring was gray, the only available energy was spent in the bathroom, and I wasn't capable of even carrying on a conversation with him. My mood swings were high-high or so low as to be dangerous, and my irritability was unbelievable.

Several very uncomfortable tests proved that nothing alien was robbing me of my health. No, indeed! The real thief could not be cut off because I carried her around in my head, giving refuge when others asked her to give up her hold or pillage, her lies.

Ron was at least relieved to know I wasn't dying of cancer, which was his number one suspicion. The doctors could only say I was too thin and that they didn't understand bulimia. I could have told him about the binging and purging before the time, my discomfort, and our money were spent, but I was still very much "in the closet." Neither of us understood the ever-present emotional volcano that was even then building up for another eruption. Besides, I always believed "the binge before" was clearly the last one I would have again, and I was always at the end of my nightmare.

Ron's well-meant feedback was to cause me to eat even more. It was time to take another gulp and plunge into one of the other symptoms of bulimia, the purging. More confusion, more helplessness. Then he discovered bloody bandages in the bathroom and I had to confess to using them to pad my tailbone. I used them because there was no cushion of fat to protect my pants from rubbing and causing it to bleed. At the time of application, I had thought it was further proof of my willpower and control, but to him it was just gross. When I looked at his disbelieving face, I knew he was right. Now we both knew I had a serious illness that had to be stopped!

With my secret out once and for all, I half hoped he would be willing to assume the nonvirtuous role of policeman, but thank God, he couldn't and wouldn't. He refused to play the game or be my watchdog. The few times he did, I became furious and a perpetual round of hide and seek would occur. I'd wait until he left the house or was outside, then I'd eat all the leftovers. Or I'd refuse to eat anything at all when he would suggest perhaps I was eating a little too fast, or too much.

Eating enough for three before bringing in the family's portion was a favorite trick, as well as picking everyone's plate clean before washing the dishes. Poor Ron, he simply was not meant to be my father. It was a terrible position to put him in and not at all fair. My control was beginning to look childish and harmful to me.

TWELVE
DR. JEKYLL AND
MR. HYDE

Having breakfast at a local pancake house with friends, I decide, *I'll just have grapefruit and one soft-boiled egg. Pancakes are so heavy, and I can't stand that sweet syrup.*

Later that same day, in the car on the way home: *I want candy, and I want it now! I'll stop by the fast food market and buy one of every kind they have. Maybe a big bag of toffee nuts and a quart of ice cream to wash it down, I can't wait! Why is everyone in my way? Why can't traffic move faster!*

Jekyll and Hyde, Jackie and who? Was it feasible to look in a mirror and see only one person, one set of values, one personality—only to walk to the kitchen or meet friends for breakfast and change into a Hyde personality? Perhaps I could have accepted all of me gorging, or all of me fasting, but what was unacceptable was eating practically nothing, only later in the same day to go out of my way to binge. It was unacceptable to spend good money on bad junk food, or literally to clean out the kitchen cupboards and settle for leftovers just on the verge of going bad!

Allow me to digress for a moment's clarification

before continuing my Jekyll and Hyde comparison. My husband, Ron, had publicly disclosed my slight indiscretion with "suspect" food. He was asked in a television interview to enlarge on his initial awareness of my illness. Without a moment's hesitation, he launched into the time he reached for his favorite cookie box only to pull out strange, smaller cookies than he was used to seeing—my laxatives. The audience roared; he felt the exhilaration of successfully being "on," and continued to share the time I ate what he called "green food." By this time the audience was all his. He was grinning from ear to ear, and I was praying for a commercial! I really couldn't be too angry though; after all, he had been through it with me. Laughter and a sense of humor have become a relaxing part of our life style and definitely a prerequisite for survival. But in front of thousands of viewers?

Now, in my defense, allow me to take the opportunity to clear my name. Only once did I ever think about eating anything "green." A small cheesecake, maybe a little fuzzy around the edges with an ever-so-light green hue, which I carefully scraped off before diving into the cream cheese delight. Trust me on this, I really did scrape off the growth, and I did not, I repeat, did not eat the fuzzy foliage!

Now that that's off my chest, let's get back to the Jackie and who dilemma. The truth is, trying to understand and clarify *one* identity was scary enough for one lifetime. Did I actually now dare to acknowledge another? Two identities seemed ludicrous and beyond scary to bizarre, but nonetheless, it felt like having a set of "unidentical" twins living inside me. The switch from one to the other was not just an emotional one, but physical as well. Pretty hard to deny and ignore the change from a calm, thin, flat-stomached appearance of one twin to that of the other—complete with a glazed expression and swollen eyes from sugar deposits (sporting a huge stomach and an overwhelming desire to stay in the playpen and play with her toys). And what of everyone else? That is what my life was like, everything changing on the inside, everything changing on the outside.

Was I opening a door I couldn't close? In deciding to work with my "two of me" theory, was I really only planting a bad seed? Ignoring the separation in my mind, trying to pretend it didn't exist would not keep my two sides from destroying the battlefield—my body. I couldn't let that happen without at least a stab at peaceful coexistence, even if that meant a fight.

Crazy or not, I felt as if there were two of me crowded into the same body. Rather than being in a peaceful cohabitation, the warring twosome seemed to hate each other. Their objective appeared to be getting rid of the other. It was a continual war with no generals, no direction—only blindly led infantry with loaded weapons, all aimed at destroying me.

These two sides of my personality didn't seem to ever be of one mind, so I had to take the leap and see them as separate identities in order eventually to join them as one. I was sick to death of eating nothing one minute, and everything the next. I was sick of crying my eyes out in the morning just to become a stone encasement in the evening. Facing the separation of my personality was becoming urgent; I wanted to get out, once and for all.

It was only when I was first able to face the separation in my mind that I could bear to allow it to unfold and flow through in my writing. I felt I was going to have to face the reason for the division. That could mean having to admit to a lot of dishonesty and avoidance in my life, but I needed to discover how the war had continually been fed. I wanted to cut off its food supply, literally, and one way was to transfer the battlefield to another location: my writing. I needed a better perspective as to what and who the enemy was from a more neutral territory.

In my past torment, I hadn't been able to feel above the loud roar of the ongoing struggle. I prayed that my writing could continually slow the battle down enough for me to think, feel, and begin my strategy for the next attack. What a relief to finally get it out of me once and for all. I had no idea as yet just where this gut honesty would lead me, but I knew I was no longer as afraid of going forward as I was of going backward. That itself was progress of sorts, and for the time being, it was enough. I was exhausted.

Determination mustered and rest acquired, I plunged into the dissection of my mind. I faced the fact that there were two of me being housed within one very weak frame. Both were trying, in a very crowded and cramped condition, to win the battle for control. Just facing the separation had to be enough for awhile, because there was absolutely no way I could or would communicate with that part of me that was binging. I hated her and wished her dead, but didn't know how to commit the dirty deed without killing both of us! I was still frightened of planting the bad seed, but the alternative of never being able to stop the binger, or know when she would take over and hurt both of us, was much more frightening.

If you are now ready to take the same "leap," then pull up a chair, and get comfortable. Believe it or not, this could be the beginning of the rest of your life; it was for me.

I imagined there was a thick wall right down the center of my personality. It did not divide good and evil, but higher and lower. Neither one could hurdle this wall to reach the other. As I was imagining the concrete barrier, I tried to feel myself in the higher state. That is where I was at the time, because I wasn't binging. I tried to feel what being in the higher felt like—to experience being there. I heard nothing but a single word—safe. Safe because I wasn't hungry beyond a normal appetite. Safe because the binger wasn't in control.

Then I tried to relax and communicate with the lower—nothing. No matter how hard I concentrated, nothing. Why? Was she truly too stupid to do anything but eat? Wait a minute. I wasn't born with this separation, or at least I don't think I was; therefore, I rationalized, I had to give her permission to separate and exist. Why couldn't I communicate with her when I chose to and what was she protecting so vehemently?

First, I tackled *why*. It stands to reason that if I allowed the separation, indeed instigated it, it must have been in an effort to protect myself from any discomfort I didn't feel "up" to dealing with. Therefore, I gave the lower permission to exist, but not to speak. I didn't want her to do anything but binge! If I had wanted exposure, I'd have had a roll of film developed! That's why, from the higher, I could read Bible verses that enabled me to feel so confident, so sure God had a better way and the power to share that same better way with me. I believed God from the higher—each time swearing to read the faith-producing passages to the lower when the next binge cycle roared like a lion.

But it always fell on deaf ears. The lower refused to absorb, hear, or trust the Bible or God. She never said so. She never said anything. She just mindlessly took over, running into the playpen, into her own world of dishonesty and avoidance, to her waiting toys. She was a reflex of my own making—created to cope the only way she knew how—by binging and purging.

First order of business? Give my lower permission

to speak, permission to comprehend and understand the higher. In the meantime, she was communicating in her own way—through binging and purging. There was no doubt that when she was present she was hard to ignore! If I could encourage her to think more, actually speak during the cycles, then understanding was bound to follow, trusting one another a strong possibility, and merging inevitable.

Now for the *what*. The secret my lower was protecting was the volcano of hidden and undealt with emotions. It was her sole purpose to alleviate the erupting pressure of the too-full and overflowing volcano of lava. Every time she gorged, she was tamping the dreaded and uncomfortable feelings back down again into the volcano. It took an enormous amount of food to defuse the pressure, and each eruption seemed to require even more food than the time before—with the eruption cycles coming closer and closer together.

When did this volcano begin forming? During my childhood. I had submerged all the feelings that I had decided very early might hurt me, incapacitate me, or cripple me. If I showed weakness, no one would want me, everyone would turn from me. I couldn't escape negative feelings, but I could steer clear of them in the future. I could count on one hand the number of boys I had dated as a teenager. The rejection of my first boyfriend at age thirteen was too uncomfortable to want to repeat. I would avoid any form of rejection from that day on, even if it meant never dating or sharing myself with anyone again.

Anger—how do you tell yourself at age ten that you're really only mad at yourself for needing so much approval from others in order to justify your existence? I didn't realize that to do so was instilling in myself a huge hatred for any form of imposed control. Control meant tying my hands so I couldn't defend myself, my values, principles, opinions. So whenever I was challenged either to be myself or succumb to another's control, I became angry. I was too frightened to be myself, but hated the control I was giving over to others because of my fear. So I inflicted control on myself. I put myself in a prison cell and then threw away the key. I was mad at me! I pushed rejection, anger, resentment, all feelings of responsibility down, creating a volcano. In doing so, I was disclaiming all responsibility for them. For years that volcano was able to remain inactive by my isolation, depressions, and avoidance games. But later, when there was no other alternative but to erupt from the inside out, or explode on the inside and die, avoidance was no longer feasible.

My lower was going to erupt, like it or not, unless I dealt with those feelings by accepting the responsibility of their existence, and found a place to put them.

It took a long time to get the lower to communicate with the higher at any other time than during a binge—which is why it was so important not to demand that I never binge again. I was guaranteed she was in control, available for comment, when binging.

I enabled her, the lower, to continue her playpen fantasy as long as she understood she had a voice and my permission to feel as well as alleviate the volcanic pressure by binging. For awhile, she wouldn't say anything, struggling to deny she could now speak up. Just as the word "safe" came from the higher, the word "anger" came from the lower.

I didn't understand, but neither did I judge her for feeling. More binging, more trying—finally, the lower trusted my genuine wish to know her just enough to bridge the communication gap at a time other than during a binge. Just as the lower had earlier dis-

91

closed on paper her desire and need for the food, I was now actually having a conversation with her about why, and talking out loud!

Higher: *Why do you have to binge and purge?* Lower: *How dare you tell me what to do. Who do you think you are? At least I know how to make myself feel better—at least I know how to alleviate the pressure. How do you make yourself feel better? What do you do that is fun? How do you get rid of pressure? And just what does "safe" mean anyway? What kind of a feeling is that? Is that what you expect me to do, feel safe for the rest of my life? What kind of comfort is that? Until you can come up with some alternatives and choices other than binging, don't bother me— just leave me alone, you hypocrite.*

Wow! It was enough to make me wonder who was the bad guy and who was the good guy! At least my lower was honest. What did that make the higher?

From that day on, I could not hate my lower. It was obvious both higher and lower had a long way to go, and one was not more to blame than the other. They both were going to have to be willing to learn more about the other in order to grow together and merge. To try to understand and forgive the lower was not to be the martyr. Indeed, I prayed the lower would agree to let the higher in on her innermost secrets, her feelings. It made it so much easier when I could put the condemnation and guilt aside.

I'm not claiming my life was easy from that time on. It wasn't. Let's go back to patience—the annoying but necessary ingredient trait to recovery. Conversing on a regular basis from higher to lower was slowly forthcoming. But still the binging and purging were hard to accept. My progress would slow to a leak as the binges continued with annoying regularity, even with the constant insight of my writings, conversations, and the honesty of my motivation. My days

92

evolved into a harlequin comedy: throw a tantrum, catch a nap, write a lot, eat a lot, purge awhile, cry awhile. Somehow, recovery wasn't progressing as easily or as quickly as I thought it should.

To demand of myself that I never binge or purge again, was only to set myself up for more failure, and the next binge-purge cycle. Obviously, I was living proof that there was no such animal as an isolated bulimic cycle. The cycles were going to overpower me again and again. The lower did not automatically relinquish her hold and carelessly give her trust to the higher, just because the higher had condescended to acknowledge her presence in the scheme of things. Could I be satisfied to grow through the binges with my newfound weapon—communication? Could I become patient enough to allow the eventual merging? Before learning to walk, I would have to be content to crawl.

THIRTEEN
THE LITTLE GIRL
INSIDE

As my lower self cautiously confided in my higher self, I became aware of her childishness. I don't mean that in a derogatory way, but in a literal sense. She was easily hurt, easily angered, and easily confused. She appeared to be a bundle of emotions. She had not only negative feelings, but positive ones as well; only she had no ability to cope with them. She was all of my feelings: not just anger, or selfishness, but also compassion, warmth, and caring. I was sensing the impossibility of existing in the higher alone. I needed my lower to temper the rigidity of expected perfection demanded by the higher.

As an example of this rigidity and lack of compassion from the higher, one of the girls I counsel had not binged for a month. She was feeling pretty confident, but living in the higher only. She had managed to go into the higher and stay, by exerting tremendous self-control as opposed to being able to relax and therefore not need to binge. As such, the lower's existence was ignored, denied altogether. Functioning without her lower's compassion, she wasn't facing any of her lower's needs, only ignoring them.

Having lunch with a bulimic girl friend who was asking for her help and understanding in dealing with her own binging, she was unable to help. She became very impatient with her friend, saying, "If you won't follow my advice when I tell you how to help yourself, then you'll just have to get better on your own!" She was angry with her friend for not being able to quit the binging as she had done. By ignoring the lower and the compassion she could have offered from having been there herself, she was temporarily stronger, but not nicer. She was firmer in her conviction never to binge again, but weaker in her tolerance. The next day she binged. Her lower did not let her get away with it! After all, to judge a friend meant to judge herself also. Our higher self tries to be rigid and tough as a defense against the always present fear of the lower's control.

There were times when my "child" would test my higher. I would be trying to assure her of my sincerity in loving her, no matter how long it took to convince her, and still binge. I could hear her tease me with "Do you still love me?" It took a lot of patience to reassure her after 30,000 calories, but I kept trying, constantly forgiving the two of us over and over again, until she could see from experience that I wouldn't turn my back on her.

We need both higher and lower to function, to balance ourselves, to recover from bulimia. But my lower's emotions were childish and that confused me. I tried to see the lower in my mind, to picture her "tuning out" and swallowing her feelings rather than experiencing them. I realized the volcano had been building since that first isolation incident, and denial as well as avoidance had become so natural. It felt normal to continue into my seemingly unaccountable depressions, and undefined as well as unclaimed anger.

I was that little girl! Emotionally, I was still about thirteen years old. How embarrassing to be running around in a woman's body, and never reacting to situations beyond a young girl's emotional range. Was it possible to grow up according to my adult years? Of course, it was! Remember, facing the trial is always half the battle.

First things first. She didn't want anyone else's attention or understanding—she wanted mine, from the higher. She didn't care about the higher's parents, she wanted me to be her parent. And she was open to alternatives other than binging and purging—just as long as I wasn't that absentee parent anymore. For years my lower had been condemned by me for her childishness, her immaturity. In my embarrassment over her, I was the abusive parent that was never there when she needed me. She was tired of being alone and neglected.

My higher had to evolve to the parent, and my lower became my child. She, the child in me, wasn't bad, she was just a frightened little girl with no one to love her, care for her, or help her grow up to merge with my higher, my parent.

It was a strange place to be at first, but the more I thought about it, the more it made sense.

No wonder I was afraid of her expressing any anger. A young child if provoked is capable of killing. The child's anger is all consuming, and mine had been in that volcano, festering for years. I was terrified that the anger might be released. I feared I might actually kill someone! Better to keep it under wraps? No! Once I understood what I was dealing with, I began to see the necessity of directing the expression of these emotions from the higher, or parent, through God. I began making up cards to help me. (You will find samples in the back of the book.) I took one feeling at a time, examining it, redefining its meaning, and discovering ways and means to express it without being afraid. Then, with the help of God, I put it where I hoped it could never again haunt me from below.

When a child is very small, he doesn't understand the God concept; Mom and Dad are gods for awhile. Some of my clients have been physically abused as children. Even though Emily (not her real name) was petrified of her mother's anger and abuse, she still wouldn't tell anyone what was happening to her. She loved her mother, her god, and assumed she had to be somehow deserving of the beatings she was getting. If Mom was God, how could it be her fault if she disciplined Emily? Emily was obviously being such a bad little girl, Mom had to hurt her. As unhappy as Emily was, she felt a certain amount of security in her pain. Home and Mom were still safer than the dark, the unknown future. Her now was all she had as a security blanket. She certainly didn't want to give up that security. Although life was painful, what guarantee did she have that the future held anything better? Besides, all she had to do was be a better girl, quit provoking the beatings, fit in better, and achieve goodness. Then Mom would love her and not hurt her.

Emily's binging and purging were "safe." As horrible as the cycle was, as distasteful as it was to her, she was afraid to give it up. What guarantee would she have of replacing it with something better? Binging became Mom—painful, hurtful, but a security nonetheless because she knew exactly what it was going to feel like each time. It never disappointed her in its playpen appearance—going in; nor in its cage entrapment—going out. Not even the ever-accompanying guilt and anger from the higher brought a surprise. The pattern was always the same.

When we had worked together for awhile, Emily

could see she was glad Mom didn't beat her anymore. Mom was not God, therefore she was accountable for her own temper, and not exempt from being human and making mistakes. Beating Emily was a mistake. Mom was responsible for her failings, but not for eternity. She could be forgiven. It was wrong to beat Emily, but it was not Emily's responsibility to accept the guilt. Emily could forgive her mom and herself for bulimia, and also give up binging and purging. It felt good not to have to punish herself; she didn't deserve the beating by proxy, and the future was certainly better without the beatings from Mom, and the beatings from herself.

I bring Emily's example up for a reason. As a child, she valued her mother, listened to her, and believed what she was told. Mom was security, and to do away with her was to open the door to fear of the unknown. The little girl inside my body wanted her parent, me. No matter how I had tried to hide from her, to get rid of her, to refuse to acknowledge her existence or listen to her, she still wanted me. My child wanted to trust me, but I never listened. I was too busy being afraid of her. Unlike my higher who had hated her because of this fear, my child loved me, the higher, but didn't know of any way to get my attention. Every time she binged or purged she was screaming for my attention and affection. Well, she finally had it, undivided and all hers!

I often wondered why my parent couldn't scare my child, nor threaten her with death. Think about it ... does a child have a sense of her own mortality? No! How do you scare a little kid with gory threats of dying with your head shoved in a toilet, or having a heart attack, or even leaving your own children motherless? You can't. You can make them feel guilty and afraid of displeasing you, but it's more difficult to instill a fear of death and eternal damnation. That was why, from my parent, I couldn't be angry enough to make her stop. I heard all the threats from my husband and others. "You're killing yourself. What am I going to tell our son when he sees his mother would rather die than face the future and his growing up?" I would feel terrible, guilty and scared! Furious, I would then repeat all this to my child, who, unable in her child's mentality to face such monumental facts and threats, quickly binged! I had to learn to see her as a child—my child. As foolish as it may sound, it was the only way. I had to want to protect and help her, not condemn and attack her; to learn to allow for her mistakes, not set up rules and regulations she couldn't accept or comprehend.

In order to discover the little girl inside, I often recommend redeeming a picture from a photo album of yourself at an age when you can most comfortably identify with your own "child." Look at different ages of your physical development until you come across the one that reminds you most of the beginning of the tuning out, or isolation period. Carry the picture around with you, looking at her often to help you identify with her, with her pain. I saw and remembered so much of my confusion when looking at one of my pictures. I couldn't believe what a difference it made!

It also helped me to relate more closely. I talked to her as if she were in front of me. Actually, she was much closer than that—inside of me. Merging is much more successful with the identification of a picture. Some even call their child by a nickname from the past, or one of their own choosing, to enable the personal relationship that is so essential.

I also ask my girls to write as much as possible from the child, when she will allow the communication. Each has had remarkable success with helping her to understand the confusion that accompanies the identification of the exposed emotions. Each feeling, in time, can then be dealt with from a more mature position and vantage point. Help from the adult to alleviate stress and fear is vital for the development of patience. Several girls have even been able to identify with their child more distinctly by placing the writing pen in their left hand.

Above all, remember, a child needs your love and understanding, and she needs God. My child was tired of being afraid of the dark, and I was tired of abusing her and forcing the darkness upon her.

FOURTEEN
LOVE ME NOW!

The parent and child must communicate and work toward a peaceful coexistence, through recognition of one another and a mutual understanding and cooperation. If not, the war will continue, indeed escalate.

Ron and I have eaten out, or brought prepared food home, nearly all of our twenty years of marriage. It was, and is, easier than preparing three different meals three times a day. Add our son, Jeff, and you have three completely different sets of taste buds. There was a time when food was the high point of the day for us. Ron worked nights, and Jeff was out of school just in time to grab a quick bite before his dad left for the evening. It was a very social and comfortable time for us. Unfortunately, as my bulimic symptoms became more pronounced, eating became a nightmare.

Ron and Jeff would sit with their menus on the table where they had been for the last ten minutes, running out of small talk or trying not to stare at me while my menu would still be plastered in front of me as if growing there. It couldn't have been easy for them not to acknowledge that I had been in the same position without saying a word for so long. In the meantime, the waitress was leering at us, her pencil rapping out a hurry-up message against her pad.

I was thinking, *No, you can't have the hot fudge sundae, you'll binge and get fat if you do. But I don't want the smelly fish. And that pasty, dry potato is awful!*

By the time I had made the wrong decision as to what to eat, my family was staring confusedly at me, the waitress was sending conciliatory, "How do you put up with her?" looks to them; and I was mad at everyone! It was Ron's fault for bringing me, Jeff's fault for not having bulimia, the waitress's for disapproving of my frustration and childishness, and mine for being so crazy in the first place! By the time the food arrived—the object of my affection and only reason to rise in the morning—I was furious! No matter what I chose, it was offensive to the other half of me. If it was a sundae, the parent was fit to be tied because she didn't win out with the fish. If I had the fish, the child was beside herself and feeling cheated. I could barely eat anything. I was mad at everyone, and confused as ever.

Obviously, the child wanted the hot fudge sundae, and the parent wanted the safe food.

The necessity to be as honest about the separation as possible was continually brought home to me by the repetition of such incidents—the battle for control.

The lower me may have been a child emotionally, but she also possessed a child's innocent and accurate perception of the truth. She definitely had my number, and was letting me know it loud and clear in no uncertain terms. Acknowledging her existence did not instantly produce the maternal instinct in me.

It would have to grow gradually. We had to become a comfortable habit with one another, but this could only begin when I could admit, *I don't love you today, but God willing, with some hard work, I will tomorrow.*

If I wanted to get well, I was going to have to realize that recovery necessitated the recognition of the little girl inside as an integral part of myself; she was not on the sidelines watching and wondering what I was thinking, hoping to be called on for her opinion. She was in on what was really being thought and felt. She knew the truth, and was perceptive enough to feel crummy when I tried to fake the relationship. That meant I would have to be honest with both of us. I would have to take the responsibility of learning from the child by listening to her feelings and then help her.

From the parent I needed to understand when the need to hide first took place and why. Then together, parent and child, we would decide how to deal with those same feelings.

Now we all know my story—I hate control! Was I now dooming myself to just another control from within?

Accepting responsibility was not exactly my strong point. Avoiding feelings was another way to avoid being responsible for them. Now I was asking myself to acknowledge and accept a very demanding responsibility. The raising of my child within was an awesome undertaking, and one I had been continually trying to avoid.

I have a son, therefore I am a parent in a very literal sense. When he was a small boy, I never allowed temper tantrums, and I believed in spanking when necessary. His desires were always contingent on his needs and on my ability and willingness to give. In other words, I was bigger than he was! But in dealing with the lower me, I felt incapacitated! I couldn't get my hands on her! It seemed to me that she was holding a loaded gun to my head—*Love me now, or I'll binge!*

There was no way to hand the responsibility to someone else, nor was it possible to get rid of her. I couldn't refuse to accept her as mine; just as I couldn't give the dreaded symptoms to someone else, stop them as the parent, or deny their inevitability.

I had reached a solid wall—the same wall that separated parent and child. It was impossible to accept the theory, the separation, without accepting the lower. It was a package deal, all or nothing.

How to go about it? Stop faking a relationship and love I didn't as yet feel! I was going to have to *want* to love her, *want* to get to know her, *want* to want her. I wasn't fooling her, so why try to fool me!

Again, during my mindless years of binging and purging, my parent and child never seemed to merge, never seemed to penetrate the wall. That would have first revealed one to the other; second, it would have enabled an awareness of their separateness; and third, it would have allowed the identification with one another's pain and confusion.

As gross as the bulimic cycles were at the time, it was a physical merging of sorts. It was the one time when the two sides of my personality did anything at the same time, physically and tangibly.

More and more I recognized my child to be an invaluable piece of the puzzle. We had to begin working together toward recovery, but accepting her from my weak parent role seemed a huge responsibility. I couldn't absorb the responsibility from my parent completely without her help.

Even with the admission and willingness, it was still hard! I spent much of my time confused. Every new situation was weighed, mulled over, and still, half the time, misunderstood! Why? What was I missing?

I truly believe everyone to some degree has a child-like version of himself trapped inside, trying to be heard. Bulimics do not have the market cornered. It's just that, in our case, the parent is as opposed as the child to accepting the responsibility of the exposure of her hidden volcano. Both are afraid of any and all responsibility, even though it is required just to exist. For me, this was always out of a fear of not performing the responsibility perfectly and thus failing.

My child, once I had given her permission to communicate, was forced to be on her own, responding the only way she knew how, until the parent could accept the responsibility for her. This is what the child really wanted and was craving.

We are both parent and child. As long as we can be aware of the two perceptions and the need for the child to wait for the parent to react first, and explain later, merging is sooner in coming.

This will occur more and more as the parent realizes that the child is not only capable, but willing to help in the merging process. This aids the delegation of responsibility. The parent does not have to carry the load alone, nor does the child. I call this cooperative growth. It involves leaning on one another, discovering that both halves can and must work together in order to begin recovery.

Jekyll and Hyde? If so, maybe Mr. Hyde just didn't have an enlightened, understanding parent in Dr. Jekyll.

Betty has vomited every morning for the past ten years. "Why, I can't seem to stop! I have to start my day by eating just enough to vomit. I hate it, but can't stop it."

When we talked, I asked when she was making time for her little Betty inside.

"Well, the only time is when I come to see you. It's a long way to your house, and I talk to her all the way here and back. What has that to do with anything?"

I remember when my own son, Jeff, was a baby. I spent a lot of time in the bedroom crying because he was in the kitchen, the farthest room away from my bedroom, screaming. He sensed my inadequacy where he was concerned, and yet he demanded my attention. If the only way to get the attention was to scream, then scream he would! I'll never forget the day I gazed down into those squinty brown eyes as he was about to let loose with another round of ear-busting screams. Suddenly, in the midst of the chaos, I loved him—I really did! I picked him up because I wanted to! I learned a valuable lesson from the experience. I started picking him up at times other than when he was crying. He learned to respond to my efforts—to receive my love unconditionally. He learned that he didn't have to do anything to receive it—certainly not cry.

Even today, now that he is seventeen, I make time for Jeff, no matter what is happening. We take the time to be together. Jeff and I have breakfast together every morning, no matter what. It's our time. As a teenager, he needs to know that Mom's attention is given because I need to be with him. I need to show my love, and receive his for me—I want that, and so does he. We don't earn one another's love, but try to give it freely. There is no doubt in my mind that if we didn't have this time together, and share an unconditional love for one another, he would find a way—conscious or unconscious—to get love any way he could. At his age, a really good way would be to fail his classes (that would definitely get my attention). Whether it be positive "strokes" or negative ones, he would demand the recognition and do whatever it took to receive it!

When it comes to the mother and child relationship, the child knows no pride. It's you she wants and you she'll have.

I advise my girls to set up a time, to make an appointment, if you will, to be with the little person inside yourself. Betty's child knew that every Friday on the way to see me and back, she had her parent's attention. In order to keep that attention, she had to keep causing Betty to come. That meant to vomit. Also, if the only way to ask for this recognition of her needs during the day was to vomit every morning, then the little Betty inside would do it. It was the child's way of trying for her parent's attention and love.

Now, as she makes time during the day, even for only ten minutes, for her child, Betty's parent and child are learning to trust one another more. The little girl is seeing that Betty, the parent, is caring enough to give her unconditional concern, if not yet love, at a time other than the vomiting.

This will help when receiving the two responses at the same time during a situation or conflict. The child has to learn to *trust* the parent, even though she already loves her. The parent has to learn to field the responses first, before the child reacts emotionally in anger as a defense. If the child knows the parent is absorbing, dissecting, and evaluating situations in order to protect her, she will be more cooperative. Soon the child will be trustful enough to hear it, believe it, and be soothed by it.

Marcia is a middle-aged woman who lives 500 miles from her parents. She was not a very happy young girl while living with them and couldn't wait

107

to move out on her own. She thought she would feel an immediate release and relief from the separation. Her life would then really begin. Unfortunately, Marcia couldn't move far enough away. She carried Mom and Dad's control around in her mind where the "tape" played continually, haunting and ruling her every move. She lived her life just as rigidly as if they were standing in front of her.

It took quite a while before she could enable herself to relax and create her own more lenient tape that reflected her true identity. She had been binging and purging in defiance of the tapes of control without understanding why.

One way I was able to help her see the correlation between her real parents and that running tape of control, was to show her the parent and child inside herself. Upon discovery of the child within, she was then able to see how she, the parent, was emotionally abusing the little girl inside herself just as her own parents had abused her emotionally. In freeing her child from the control bondage, she was able to free herself as the parent, and forgive her own parents for being human. Seeing herself do the same thing to her child within, without even being aware of it, helped her to be more tolerant of Mom and Dad's vulner- abilities as parents themselves. She is now able to see them without hating them, because she is no longer afraid of their control over her. She is tolerant with her little girl within, forgiving of her parents, and free to be herself.

Accepting the responsibility of being a parent to my child inside became easier as I practiced it and was able to care for her more and more. Eventually, I was able to say *I love you*—and mean it. From then on, it was a responsibility I welcomed—a responsibility I could live with!

FIFTEEN
GUILTY?

Mirror, mirror on the wall: Am I going to hell because I binge and purge? How's that for a crummy "what-if?" Whom does the mirror on the wall reflect anyway? God? My family's supposed condemnation and judgment? Myself as the parent? Or, maybe my child within? Who? Just how guilty am I? By whose standards?

Now for the good stuff! Yes, you heard me correctly. Exposing assumed guilt is a terrific step! Once feelings have been shown the light of day, you have defused them of their scare potency. So many times the fear is of exposure itself, in the way the revelation will occur.

Guilt also needs to see the light of your understanding, your determination to be free. I couldn't wait to get rid of the guilt feelings and all their pressure!

I have, as best as I could up to this point, explained much of the mechanics involved in the recovery stages of bulimia, as well as the original breakdown that made the repairs necessary in the first place.

With all my heart, I do not believe that I would have been healed without the miraculous work of my Lord and Savior, Jesus Christ.

I have not set out to write a testimony. However, I would like to share my own faith, which was an important part of my recovery.

I will say at the outset that permanent relief was made available to me only when I called upon the greatest physician of all—Jesus Christ. I learned that my trial was to bring me back to my God for all the right reasons: in order to teach me, to show me forgiveness from the Master, and as a bonus to reveal a formula for my recovery that could have come from no other doctor on earth.

Ten years prior to the final symptoms of bulimia, binging and purging, I had asked God to forgive me my sins and live in my heart in the form of the Holy Spirit. I was "born again," but I hadn't dedicated my life to him, nor had I specifically asked him to direct me toward his will for me. Oh, I had submitted to lip service through confession of the words . . . but because I didn't understand the depth and real meaning of such confessions, I wasn't ready. Bulimia was a huge trial because it had been gaining in volume and momentum for so many years. The bigger the trial or need, the greater his wisdom and comfort. Believe me, it didn't always seem that he was on my side, or that I was on his. Growth is painful. I had to be ready for its inevitability as well as its blessings.

On to the guilt. I can well remember, sometime into my five-year mindless period, crawling into a corner of my bedroom, folding my arms around myself (actually feeling a comfort of sorts), and sobbing over and over again.

"I'm guilty, I'm guilty. I'm so very . . . very . . . guilty." My son walked into the room, and upon seeing and hearing me, asked, "Of what, Mother? What have you done that you are so guilty of?"

I didn't know what to tell him and I didn't understand myself. In fact, I hadn't even realized what I was declaring so pathetically, but I knew I felt guilty. I was absolutely overwhelmed by its condemnation and futility. It was as if it were whipping me physically and I had no recourse but to submit. I felt it deep down in the core of my existence. I was guilty!

Another time, and again in the bedroom, my husband discovered me sitting in my chair with my arms wrapped around myself in an embrace . . . rocking back and forth.

"What are you doing, Jackie?" he asked. Until I opened my mouth, I didn't know. Sometimes I wish I could be outside my own body, holding, soothing, and comforting myself. Conveying to myself a reassurance that everything was going to be all right.

Ron puzzled. "Let me hold you, honey. I want to love you. Won't you let me do that much for you?" I wished I could, I really did. But I felt like only I could love me the way I wanted to be loved. I didn't understand why, but if I could do it myself there wouldn't be any attachment, any commitment that would come from the fear of having to deliver or fulfill.

I was so frightened by the admission to Ron and Jeff and to myself that I didn't have time on either occasion to feel stupid—only shocked by such an exposure of vulnerability.

I have always felt and been guilty! To be a bad Christian witness made me feel guilty. To have no mind of my own made me feel guilty. To let that girl from my childhood talk me into exposing myself before the entire student body and make a fool of myself made me feel guilty. Always fitting in made me feel guilty! Guilty! Guilty! Guilty for feeling bad, and guilty even for feeling good. Goodness knows I had no reason or right to be happy; there had to be a catch in there somewhere.

Feeling guilty actually kept me from getting better for years. But what was I really saying? Why couldn't

I rectify the problem myself and go ahead with my life? If I felt under such condemnation from myself, then obviously I was never forgiving myself for anything. If I can't forgive myself, then it must be because I don't believe God forgives me either. First then, before I can forgive myself, I will have to find out if God really forgives me.

Let's see now ... I've been a Christian for ten years. I know I bought a Bible ... it must be here some place. . . . But ten years is a long time to misplace something. Ah, here it is! Now ... egads! Am I going to have to read the whole thing before I can find out if God forgives me or not? Wait a minute, don't panic ... the concordance at the back ... that will surely help speed things up a little ... let me see now ... ah— great!

"My little children, I am telling you this so that you will stay away from sin. But if you sin, there is someone to plead for you before the Father. His name is Jesus Christ, the one who is all that is good and who pleases God completely. He is the one who took God's wrath against our sins upon himself, and brought us into fellowship with God; and he is the forgiveness for our sins, and not only ours but all the world's" (1 John 2:1, 2).

How wonderful. He's speaking directly to the child inside me. First, he tells me that sin is wrong, then he lets me know that he is aware that I will sin again. But because of Jesus and his willingness to be a living sacrifice for my sins, I am by his grace forgiven.

There is no doubt whatsoever in my mind that I was healed of bulimia when I first asked to be—not because I was worthy of the healing, or because I had worked harder than others to be healed, but because I had been forgiven. I was forgiven for not bringing the guilt and condemnation to him in the first place. Forgiven for exerting my own self-control to such an extent as to alienate myself from him more and more. I was healed by his grace and forgiveness in order to grow from the experience, the pain, and the suffering. I had to be willing to stop judging myself guilty because I was never going to forgive myself or feel worthy enough.

It's like waiting to have a baby until you can afford one ... you never can. I was never going to be perfect enough, or achieve enough to deserve the healing.

Ephesians 6:18 says: "Pray all the time. Ask God for anything in line with the Holy Spirit's wishes. Plead with him, reminding him of your needs, and keep praying earnestly for all Christians everywhere."

I know in my heart it was in line with the Holy Spirit's wishes for me and all bulimic men and women to be healed. The dividing wall is the inability to accept that healing and his forgiveness. I had to *allow* the healing, and that took time, just as it took time to learn to accept his forgiveness. He's very patient and very understanding.

I also felt a good deal of release from "praying earnestly for all Christians everywhere." You bet! I prayed that they would be more understanding of my bulimia and lack of communication as to how I was feeling and then expressing myself. Selfish? I never said I was perfect.

It says in Matthew 5:13: "You are the world's seasoning, to make it tolerable. If you lose your flavor, what will happen to the world?"

Tell me that isn't ointment on the old wounds! That's you, and that's me ... everyone in Christ! To me, it means he wants us to be victorious! I couldn't begin to live a victorious life in Christ until I could dump this miserable guilt over bulimia and take up my Christian walk once and for all!

I began to see guilt as my enemy: a cop-out that kept me from getting better. As long as I hung onto my unworthiness, I was declaring for all the world to see and hear that God would not forgive me my sins, God did not want me to get well, God did not love me. Baloney! Of course, I was guilty. Of course, I was sinful. I was born into both and will always struggle with sin in one way or another.

Just about the time I get through cleaning my "house," one room at a time, I have to go back and start all over again. I'll never be through cleaning my house, and God doesn't insist that I be.

I think Galatians 5:16-18 says it all: "I advise you to obey only the Holy Spirit's instructions. He will tell you where to go and what to do, and then you won't always be doing the wrong things your evil nature wants you to. For we naturally love to do evil things that are just the opposite from the things that the Holy Spirit tells us to do; and the good things we want to do when the Spirit has his way with us are just the opposite of our natural desires."

To me, that means he is kind enough to acknowledge my sinful ways because he knew they were and are there, and he forgives me anyway. All the while, he is showing me ways to overcome that evil nature— not how to be perfect, but how to overcome through his perfection, and how to grow to be a happier person. There will always be new trials, new challenges. Perfection was simply never in the game plan. If he didn't expect perfection in me, then I certainly couldn't afford to expect it in myself. This was all new to me. To get better meant to stop trying for perfection in my Christian walk. I surely wasn't attaining it, then or now—only growing farther and farther from Jesus because of my elusive and impossible quest for perfection. Guilt was the enemy that kept me that quivering bowl of jelly; so I dumped it, and so can you!

As long as you stay in a corner confessing that you

are guilty, you are only condemning yourself to more guilt, stagnation, and going backward. You must believe that Jesus has already died so that you can go beyond the guilt to victory through him.

Mark 7:15, 18, 20 says: "Your souls aren't harmed by what you eat, but by what you think and say! Can't you see that what you eat won't harm your soul? For food doesn't come in contact with your heart, but only passes through the digestive system. It is the thought-life that pollutes. For from within, out of men's hearts, come evil thoughts of lust, theft, murder, adultery, wanting what belongs to others, wickedness, deceit, lewdness, envy, slander, pride, and all other folly. All these vile things come from within; they are what pollute you and make you unfit for God."

The sin of bulimia is not in the symptoms. The only sin is in not facing the real reasons for bulimia, looking at them, finding the sin in them, and then acting. You need to trust Jesus enough to allow him to correct the symptoms and cleanse you of them. The sin is fearing to put the guilt behind you and daring to give him that "thought life" once and for all.

It was sinful for me to stay in that corner of my bedroom, quivering and muttering over and over how guilty I was when I already knew and believed Jesus had died for my guilt, forgiven me my sins, and was waiting for me to allow him to heal me. I faced it, asked for forgiveness and insight, dumped any further guilt—and got on with my recovery.

Next, the rocking back and forth. I wanted an unconditional love that I didn't feel anyone on earth could give me. If I could have found it, I would have crawled back into my mother's womb and been nourished without having to ask for it or deserve it in any way. I felt there were strings attached to accepting any form of love—another nasty responsibility that only inhibited any comfort I would allow to be given to me.

Hillary explained that she wanted to be held by her husband just because she needed a hug from time to time. "But when I ask, I feel like I am prostituting myself for affection because he then expects me to go to bed with him! So I don't ask. There are times when my little girl from within wants to be held and reassured, not asked to then perform in bed! What can I do?"

I talked to Hillary's husband on the phone. He was as perplexed as she was. He had not been aware of Hillary's little girl. When we talked about it, he could see the difference in the two personalities, in the two separate needs. For awhile, every time Hillary asked for affection, he asked who was in need of that affection. At first, she was offended. "Do I have to clarify what kind of attention I need every time?"

"Yes, for awhile you do. It's only fair that I know. How I embrace my wife is far different from how I comfort a child. It's only fair to both of us for you to tell me."

A responsibility for Hillary? You bet; and a fair one.

I also wanted unconditional love from my husband, but I didn't give him the benefit of understanding my needs because at the time I didn't know about the child within. I wanted to be loved just because I was me. I didn't want to have to perform for that need, nor have to deserve it.

I couldn't accept love from my Ron until I could first accept it from Jesus. He truly loves me unconditionally. So much so that he came to die for me, so that I could unconditionally accept love and forgiveness and accept him as God. It's still hard to completely accept his unconditional love for me without forcing myself to work for it. But when I could dump the guilt, I was more open to what I really needed, and was prepared to accept, give, and forgive the others in my life.

Matthew 18:21,22 says, "Then Peter came to him and asked, "Sir, how often should I forgive a brother who sins against me? Seven times?' 'No!' Jesus replied, 'seventy times seven!'"

Another really tacky aspect of guilt was the way it imprisoned others along with myself. Matthew 18:21, 22 showed me the importance of forgiving others as well as myself, but until I could forgive *me* for absorbing others' judgment, I was not releasing them from my guilt. I must believe I can be forgiven by the people around me, that they do forgive and thus release me when I offend them. By not accepting their forgiveness of me, I am held accountable for offending them and hurting their walk with God. My job was to trust God enough to believe, "The truth will set you free; He who is free in Me is free indeed." Sometimes that would have to mean free to make mistakes and then grow from them; to release others to do the same. By exposing myself more and more, I was allowing Jesus to clean me up the right way.

Incorporating these new concepts didn't happen overnight. It took time, patience, and a lot of understanding of how patient Jesus really was and is. I still can't fathom it, but I must try in order to release myself from the guilt, and to release others from my guilt. As long as I was trying, Jesus never stopped encouraging me or forgiving me. When I would resort to old patterns and tapes, he would take the time to remind me.

Isaiah 45:9, 10 says, "Woe to the man who fights with his Creator. Does the pot argue with its maker? Does the clay dispute with him who forms it, saying,

'Stop, you're doing it wrong!' or the pot exclaim, 'How clumsy can you be!'? Woe to the baby just being born who squalls to his father and mother, 'Why have you produced me? Can't you do anything right at all?'"

All right! Do it your way! God knows best! You did send your Son to save me. You did proclaim you died to release me from eternal damnation. You do forgive me my sins, and you do forgive others of their sins against me. Therefore, it is a sin for me to keep the guilt or insist that others be guilty and incapable of being also forgiven. Gotcha!

In 1 John 4:18, 19 we find: "We need have no fear of someone who loves us perfectly; his perfect love for us eliminates all dread of what he might do to us....If we are afraid, it is for fear of what he might do to us, and shows that we are not fully convinced that he really loves us. So you see, our love for him comes as a result of his loving us first."

Naturally, I still have a lot to learn about love. But it is very comforting to trust the truths for the time being until I can better implement them in my life with honesty and confidence. I know I will be able to absorb and feel that love more every day.

Nearly all of the 1,000 women I have seen thus far suffering from bulimia and anorexia have been Christians. Many of us have gone to churches and clergymen for the relief that comes from revealing ourselves, and expecting the cleansing and insight that is always forthcoming when we are honest with ourselves. I would like to help any who are interested in comforting bulimic women without heaping even more guilt on their heads. I was guilty enough inside without accepting more from the outside. I needed to be shown loving mercy and forgiveness. In order to love another person, I had to have the capacity to love myself. Before I can love myself I have to be able to accept God's love for me. I can't love anyone else, or myself until I experience his all-forgiving love and forgiveness.

When I can accept God's love for me personally, then I can allow him to speak through others when they try to help me recover. If I have not as yet been able to trust God's love for me, then everything I hear is a judgment, criticism, and more condemnation. If you truly want to help bulimics, then please offer God's love and forgiveness before you offer your judgment. It is very easy for a non-bulimic to say, "Do not binge and purge, it is sinful." Thank you for the insight and your time. However, I heard only another know-it-all trying to control me again, and all in the name of God!

Nearly everything I read from the Bible, I read from a bulimic's point of view. I constantly need to receive encouragement and insight. I receive help when I receive God's love and understanding, his wisdom and insight. I find it hard to believe he is not pleased that I seek it.

Try to understand, bulimics hate any form of *control!* Coming to Christ at first felt like another form of that same tiresome control. I would read the Bible and feel condemnation instead of love and forgiveness. I tuned out rather than submit myself to another's control. Now when I read God's Word, I comprehend his compassion and understanding. He never puts me in a box with no hope. He is my hope; he is my way out!

The Bible is a beautiful account of his perfection, but not mine. It is a *guide* to his perfection, not mine. He didn't intend for me to read it from cover to cover quickly and then never sin again. Not every word hits me right between the eyes. I can read whole chapters or just a short paragraph, and know this is

119

what he wants me to be aware of today. What I read last week will suddenly stand out, and then I know I am to practice its truth.

There is time to get better. His schedule is different from mine. I can postpone his will for me any time I choose to; that's why he left me with a will of my own. But I don't want to postpone it. I did that for far too long. I want to go onward, forward. Those we trust and respect in the church can offer their opinions and guidance, but they cannot and must not judge us by our symptoms. Like every other Christian, I can offer well-meaning help in the form of my own experience, but each one of my girls is learning something different, something very individual. Each of them is at a different place in her recovery and growth as a Christian.

Positive confession is also of tremendous value to a recovering bulimic. The Bible gives a ton of wonderful affirmatives to choose from. Once I was able to kick the guilt habit, every paragraph was forgiving, uplifting, and inspiring. The New Testament was especially uplifting with its account of the life of Jesus. I felt his strength, his compassion, his all-consuming love, his miraculous ability and desire to take care of me until I could see the light at the end of the tunnel.

SIXTEEN
A THORNY
ROSE GARDEN

I had naively assumed that finding my way into the light of Jesus Christ would mean an automatic for-ever-after happiness. Perhaps this is true for some; it was not for me.

My salvation experience was wonderful. There were no fanfares, no twenty-one-gun salute, just a peaceful sense of coming home. Corny? Who cares? Feeling I really belonged with God, as a member of his family, meant no performing, no judgment. I was finally safe. But how I chose to grow in Christ, or not grow, would determine my forever happiness.

I didn't allow myself to feel safe or forgiven for very long. Oh, I still thrilled to the parables found in the Bible and all of the assurances of love that seemed to be directed from God to me alone; but, along with the love were rules. There were promises of correction and growth through trials. Why couldn't I be a congenial robot that blindly did as she was told? I knew the answer to that before I even uttered the question. He never meant me to be a robot.

I knew salvation was free of charge, and once given could not be taken back; but I still feared his wrath, judgment, and anger when provoked. With my weakness, that could mean a lot of provocation!

I was saved, I had a reserved berth to heaven, but I was scared of—you guessed it—the *responsibility* of being a Christian. There had to be a price to pay somewhere, a hidden clause that would cancel my ticket to heaven. How could I possibly compete with all the good Christians in the world? I definitely was not worthy of his saving grace and forgiveness. Had I already been around this particular tree a few thousand times?

There I was, a brand new Christian, feeling just as guilty as ever!

Allow me to speed up the growth process just a little. My life is a life of choices—which ones I make and how I make them will determine my happiness on earth.

In 1 Timothy 3:16 we read: "It is quite true that the way to a godly life is not an easy matter. But the answer lies in Christ, who came to earth as a man, who proved spotless, and pure in his Spirit, was served by angels, was preached among the nations, was accepted by men everywhere and was received up again to his glory in heaven."

I didn't understand what "doing his will" meant— and it scared me even to think about the meaning. I didn't feel anything was in my control now. What else could I give him? My will? What will? I was a quivering bowl of jelly, blubbering to and fro in accordance with whomever I was with at the time. How do you give up *no* control in your life? Was it possible I was controlling more than I thought I was? Impossible!

In my confusion, I let my newfound beliefs fade back and down somewhere into my volcano, along with all the other responsibilities I didn't want to face.

Ron was not as yet a Christian, and it became easier not to feel like one myself, rather than to be uncomfortable with our relationship, or with our family and friends. Every now and then I would remember my commitment to God, but I continually avoided responsibility. One day I would face it, but not yet.

The day came when the binging and purging were controlling me to such an extent that I could no longer control the problem by fasting. After five mindless years, I panicked! I was a walking zombie with seemingly no mind or will of my own. People were all around me, people who loved me and would have helped if they could have. But what could they really do? They couldn't tie me down to the bed and force feed me when I was starving myself; then only to lock the cupboards with the checkbook and car keys safely inside, and remove the refrigerator when starver turned binger.

Enough! I walked into the camp of the enemy, my kitchen, and fell to my knees. *Please dear God, help me to not binge or purge again, and I'm sorry it's taken so long for me to ask for your help.* Every day for the next seven days, I didn't binge. *This is great! All I have to do is call on God and my problem is solved!* Then, on the eighth day—a binge. Worse than all the rest put together. Why? Again, I went down on my knees in the kitchen. *Why God? I asked for your help and forgiveness; and I acknowledged your presence—what else did you want from me? Oh, it's true I didn't think anymore about the reasons for the symptoms, nor did I ask you to examine my motives and help me correct them. I only wanted to be relieved of bulimia.*

What was I saying? No wonder I binged—God allowed me to have a week free of the obvious symptoms, to show me that he was capable of releasing me any time. But I also needed to see that there was much more to my getting well than just relieving me physically. I had asked for a release; not to get to know Jesus better, not to find his will for my life— simply not to have to suffer any more discomfort. The same pattern I had always chosen. I was asking him to do all the work for me and let me take the credit. To give me another quick way out—another quick fix with no strings attached. That simply wasn't going to work. I thought about my motives for recovery. I thought about what I really wanted. I wanted to get over bulimia, yes, but I wanted to do it through Jesus. I wanted it to be his strength working through me, not mine working alone.

I prayed again. *Please, dear God in heaven, I ask Jesus Christ to intercede on my behalf. I don't understand fully the words necessary to help me, nor do I believe that in just saying them I will allow you to set me free, but I will try to understand them, try to believe and incorporate them into my life. I will seek you more often and more openly, try to trust you with my bulimia and with my life. I pray to seek your will—thy will and not mine be done. Help me to learn to understand what that means, and to learn a growth formula that will work all my life.*

I stayed on my knees until I felt insight and peace.

I began understanding that my acceptance of responsibility was a choice. I chose between an abusive and cruel existence that allowed for no mistakes, and an existence through God that promised trials and corrections but also discipline and strength, comfort and peace—forgiveness. Seen in the light of his truth and insight, the choice of responsibility was obvious, and it was becoming less frightening.

Jesus came to forgive me and you. I need to go backward from time to time in order to grow and go forward with even more of his strength and truth. *I*

*will really try, Father, to seek your will for my life
every day instead of trying to control my life in my
way. My way stunk! My way was to avoid, hide, and
hurt! Enough already!*

In 2 Corinthians 1:9 I read: "We felt we were
doomed to die and saw how powerless we were to help
ourselves; but that was good, for then we put everything
into the hands of God, who alone could save us, for he
can even raise the dead."

He never said the journey from darkness into light
would be easy or quick. Nonetheless, I felt better than
I had for a long, long time. I knew I had to begin over
again, but I no longer felt alone. It was not one
against the world—but me, the parent, me the child,
and Jesus. If I stayed in his will, I was assured the
good guys would always win. I still felt scared, but
safe—very vulnerable and very clean. So let the
merging begin!

The Bible became my nurturer and advisor. I began
consulting it often and trusting its wisdom. I could
see that a lot of the battles I had with myself were
over my so-called faults. For instance, I had considered my separation to be a terrible weakness, just as
feeling and expressing all those dirty emotions as a
girl would have been a weakness.

In reality, it takes a great deal of strength to be able
to hide one's feelings to such a degree. To bury that
much, carefully tucking it into a volcano for years, is
not easy. It requires strength and a great deal of willpower. I am not proud of having abused this strength,
nor am I claiming somehow to have developed it
myself; far from it. The credit goes to God who knew
the trials I would be asked to endure, and gave me the
strength to go through them.

To me that meant dump the guilt, and get on with
the recovery!

SEVENTEEN
HELP ME TO
HELP MYSELF

Bulimia is hardly my trial alone, and many have suffered for far longer. Having corresponded or met with over 1,000 women in the last year alone, I think I have seen just about every phase of an eating disorder there is to see. Included are those in the beginning stages of trying to control their weight as a cure-all for confusion and unhappiness, while others have been at it for twenty years, not even aware as yet that their insatiable appetite has a name.

I am the Southern California representative for Anorexia Nervosa and Associated Disorders (A.N.A.D.), a national organization based in Illinois. In this capacity, I try to facilitate as many self-help groups as I can. Through my radio and TV appearances, I have had the privilege of connecting hundreds of men and women with groups in their various areas. It has been a wonderful experience to hear from these people initially, and again after they have allowed themselves to open up with others who are suffering from eating disorders. Because it's such an isolated illness, for so many it is their first contact with a fellow sufferer.

I have had many doctors refer their patients to A.N.A.D. self-help groups as a means of helping them learn to open the lines of communication. To verbalize these feelings is very difficult, even with the doctor who is treating them.

I can remember sitting in many a doctor's office just crying, never saying a word. I didn't know how to express the pain I was feeling in any other way. It was an embarrassing show of weakness; but I couldn't help shedding tears.

A.N.A.D. was the first nonprofit, educational, and self-help organization of its kind in America. Founded by Vivian Meehan in 1975, it is dedicated to alleviating eating disorders such as anorexia and bulimia.

This dedication and determination are the reasons I wanted to be a part of their wonderfully warm and giving organization. I speak with someone from the Illinois office at least once a month. I have yet to receive anything but encouragement and a sincere attitude of caring, as well as insight into the trauma and terrible isolation of all eating disorder victims and their families. They care, and sincerely want to help.

All of A.N.A.D.'s services are free and are vitally important to the needs of those who are still asking for direction and guidance into a better life.

Although most anorexics and bulimics first show symptoms in their teens, a significant number are now in their late twenties, thirties, forties, or older. More cases are being reported in the eight-to-eleven age bracket!

A.N.A.D. needs to exist to alert our communities, our parents, our children of the dangers involved when using food as a means to a not-so-permanent and definitely unacceptable happiness. This alert must begin as soon as possible. Through the organization's efforts, millions of people are learning of these dangers; and each year thousands are assisted through A.N.A.D.'s many and diversified services.

Included in A.N.A.D.'s services are: printed materials, early detection and educational programs in communities and schools, counseling, information materials, self-help groups (for both victims and their families), and a listing of therapists and hospitals treating eating disorders. A.N.A.D. also encourages research, and the necessity at some point for a doctor's care and guidance. Many medical doctors and others in the health field endorse and support A.N.A.D. policies and services. All programs involve close association with health professionals.

Individually or in a group, it is vital first to establish everyone's ability to think rationally; and that means having enough nutritional stability to concentrate. I strongly advise victims to get a physical examination from a qualified doctor who is sympathetic to the disorder and who understands its repercussions.

Starving, vomiting, or doing both intermittently is highly vitamin-depleting. Also, one needs enough calories to enable the brain to produce adequate brain cells to permit reasonable thinking.

According to research compiled by A.N.A.D., there may be as many as 500,000 victims in this country alone (and I believe there are many more). Of these, 90 to 95 percent are women. Male cases are being reported with increasing frequency, and, in fact, I know of several myself.

I first contacted A.N.A.D. when I was recovering to such an extent that I wanted to share that recovery with others. While many A.N.A.D. groups are facilitated by various representatives of the medical community, there are also many which are being run by recovering anorexics or bulimics, as well as still very active victims trying to find a place to begin. You don't have to be totally recovered or reformed to form a group. In fact, for many sufferers, forming one is a wonderful therapy and healing process itself. For some, it is the first responsibility to be accepted for a long time. Reaching out and admitting that you are also very much in need of help is healthy, cleansing, and therapeutic.

The idea behind the groups is to help one another, not to lean upon the ones who seem to be doing better. A formula that works for one may not suit another. The idea is to share with one another, not to ask one person to fix it for everyone else.

I can't tell the members of my group how never to experience bulimia again. I can only give them the tools that will enable them to implement my ideas into their life style, using their own formula.

I have had groups fold because the leaders were receiving phone calls into the wee hours of the morning—and accepting them, because they had mistakenly assumed that as a group leader they had to. They were feeling as if they had to be at everyone's beck and call, so they once again became trapped and controlled!

We have trouble saying no to people for fear of rejection and fear of doing the wrong thing. So to be put in the position of having to make excuses for not being available, or leaving the phone off the hook, or feeling they must answer and then must come up with answers is enough to bring on the binging and purging all over again.

As members of a group, please do not ask your leader to be all things to you, to assume the responsibility of getting you better. If she feels capable, she can guide you; but constantly to expect that she fix your bulimic tendencies is only to project the same old tiring pattern that got you into this mess in the first place. You have to take responsibility for your own recovery, not ask someone to do it for you. Facing up to this is a definite step forward, and one that must be taken in order to begin getting better. If not, the members will use up the leader until there is nothing left for her to give. Please don't feed on one another. Share, ask opinions of one another, give out ideas of your own, communicate and absorb, but don't use the leader!

This is why so many A.N.A.D. groups are facilitated by doctors or someone not immediately or directly into the symptoms themselves. They can monitor what is going on, and help members stay on the right track without living their problems or being absorbed into the symptoms themselves. Many times a doctor will share the leadership role with someone in the group. This way, everyone benefits. Perhaps, if you are starting a group without the benefit of a professional's guidance, two could assume the responsibility or you could have a different leader each week. There are many possibilities.

If you cannot find a group in your area, and want to be with others, then by all means consider starting one of your own. Just be careful not to fall into the traps that would only hurt your recovery instead of initiating it.

One way to help fellow members of the group is to reach out to others by setting up a hotline among yourselves. Get used to calling one another, finding out who is available at key times. Many will find that they work the same odd hours and need help at the same odd times. They need to be communicating with one another, not calling the ones who are trying to sleep.

There is strength, a unity, a purpose in agreeing with one another, sharing your experiences, doubts, fears, and hopefully growth. There is a healing power when we gather in a mutual determination to be just as forthright as possible with each other. We can allow the luxury of seeing ourselves individually by exposing our inner selves, through the collective endeavor of a group. It is such a relief to know there are others with the same feelings of frustration and confusion, people who don't automatically think you're crazy.

In the sharing process you are opening the door to the unknown—reaching out for that door of fears, and opening it with the help of fellow members who understand and share the same fears. By daring to reach out we are shedding light on those fears together. Darkness cannot live with light. Opening a frightening can of worms alone isn't always easy or even possible. Perhaps as a group, dishonesty can be seen for what it is, and not something to be protected and guarded at any cost. Exposed and examined, a fear cannot help but lose its potency when understanding and growth are allowed via the group.

A bond will develop from the honest sharing and disclosing that will occur.

We have all spent our lives devising ways to be what others would like us to be. In doing so, we have become a false person to ourselves, a fake we don't know, respect, or love. Our image of ourselves is reflected by whomever we are with at the time. We need to devise ways to be with ourselves and love ourselves without the dreaded fear of responsibility. If a group is constantly reminding itself of this goal, it is bound to rub off. We want to learn how to be individuals and offer the same option to others. Look at the differences between yourselves, and look at ways to accept those differences without trying to change in order to fit in, or expecting the others to change.

Groups deal with emotional and physical habits,

and habits are sometimes hard to break. The longer they are allowed to dictate, the more difficult it is to decide not to allow the control. That's why constant reinforcement is necessary. You need a little help from your friends to realize your potential. We all need successes to draw from during the rough periods. Many times someone in the group will have a week of real victory. It feels good to hear that someone can and does see progress. Perhaps you can adapt that experience to your own formula. If not, at least you have had an opportunity to be encouraged and uplifted. Likewise, if you have had a good week, there is a beautiful feeling awaiting you in sharing your own victory. If having a bad week, that too has to be shared—not necessarily for the group to fix, but for comfort and encouragement.

If I may, I will offer a few suggestions as to how to direct a group toward a therapeutic session.

Decide on a topic for the week. Nothing is worse than everyone floundering with no idea as to what to say, no preparation beyond sharing their misery. A typical topic might be guilt. List all of the guilt feelings you are experiencing, and have experienced. Think about them. What do they mean to you? How has the emotion manipulated you in the past, and how does it affect you now? How do you anticipate it controlling your future? List alternatives to guilt.

When the members meet again the next week, they will have a topic that each has had an opportunity to examine, experience, and discover. Sharing will be much more beneficial and successful. Hearing how each individual deals with her concept of an emotion is very revealing. It also helps to see that there are alternative ways to handle and experience feelings and situations.

Another week you might want to introduce love as

a topic. Love is an exciting emotion, but it can be a frightening one if not dealt with by a person who first loves herself. It should not be embarrassing to care for yourself. Is it possible to share how you feel about self-love?

So many feelings are in direct conflict with love—fear, for instance. When I was angry with someone, I was generally really only frightened. I had perhaps been hurt or rejected by that someone. I was angry only as a defensive coping device to avoid the fear of the hurt or rejection. I didn't want to feel it, and was afraid it wouldn't stop hurting because I didn't know how to stop it! I was capable only of frustration over my unrecognized and unexplained anger. I knew the anger wasn't right, so I would literally swallow it, again and again, until it dissipated enough for me to be guilty only of binging and purging.

It hurt physically, so I am afraid to be physically hurt again. It was the same with emotional hurt; I was again afraid of being overpowered by the pain, and trapped by the hurt feeling inside. It was a way to live with the hurtful injury.

In two short paragraphs I have mentioned many very deep emotions . . . love, hurt, rejection, frustration, anger, guilt, and revenge. All of them are fear feelings, except for love. These emotions are so often bantered around like simple ingredients to a recipe, and with just as much casualness. In a group, feelings need to be treated with respect—examined in the depth they deserve, not just thrown around. Each person needs to understand at least his or her own interpretation of the meanings.

We need to listen to our emotions. What do they feel like? How are they manipulating us? Sometimes a good way is to listen to how others in the group deal with theirs, how they are also being manipulated by wayward and misunderstood feelings. Together, alternatives can be explored, and options uncovered to take the fear out of our feelings. Otherwise, the fear will keep the group from looking beyond to the alternatives.

There also needs to be a time when the floor is thrown open to discussion. But it does need to be monitored so that it doesn't become an endless gossip session or diet tip exchange. Given the opportunity to get off the track, some can take it as an open invitation to go back into the old avoidance pattern of not thinking beyond that next calorie.

There also needs to be a time allowed for a praise experience. This should be just before the meeting adjourns, for the purpose of allowing each person to leave on an up note (not a false high, but an encouraging ending). Ending on a downer is depressing. Everyone leaves wondering whether it was worth it. Better to leave after hearing about someone's good week, or the hope of one.

The goal of a group is to help each person to know himself or herself a little better and relate that knowledge to others in a more communicative way. These are the steps to help insure that goal:

1. Come together expecting to understand yourself.
2. Go over the previous week's assignment.
3. Openly discuss any questions that have been brought up due to the discussed assignment.
4. Perhaps have group affirmations to begin reprogramming.
5. From time to time invite a guest speaker to introduce fresh concepts.
6. Consider the establishment of a hotline, adding new extensions as different people join the group.
7. Experience a bond between members that comes only from hanging in there.

8. Have inspirational feedback to encourage one another.
9. Make next week's assignment.

How long you stay in a group is entirely up to you. Hopefully, you will become aware of your feelings, more involved, and less inclined to hide behind food. The group could become even more than a support group centering, on everyday problems and the feelings that emerge because of those problems.

There are also groups for parents of anorexics and bulimics. They may consist of parents, friends, or concerned onlookers, but they have one goal in common—helping. A.N.A.D. suggests that it is first necessary to identify the disorder. If you suspect that a child, loved one, or friend is developing anorexia or bulimia, the first step should be a visit to the physician for a thorough physical examination, or at least the encouragement to do so. Many victims will resist this move, but it is important to persist despite their protests. Require a conference with the physician. Provide the doctor with information on the following:

1. The amount of weight change over a specific period of time.
2. Changes in the menstrual period if the patient is a young woman. Has it stopped, become irregular, or *more* irregular?
3. Changes in eating behavior. For example, has the person stopped eating with the family? Is he or she eating much larger amounts of food than normal, eating only minimal amounts of food, or not eating at all?
4. Changes in personality or behavior. Has the individual become unusually withdrawn, secretive, or seclusive? Is he or she prone to tantrums? Does he or she spend a great deal of time in the bathroom

with the water running to create distracting noise while purging?

5. Don't be afraid to ask specific questions. For example, what is the physician's experience with anorexia or bulimia? How often has the physician seen this disorder?

If the physician dismisses the situation as just part of growing up, do not hesitate to seek a second opinion. Some larger cities may have hospitals with eating disorder units which could provide advice.

A.N.A.D. offers several suggestions to prevent furthering the disorder.

1. Help young people to feel good about and accept themselves, to be comfortable with who they are.
2. Provide adolescents with an appropriate but not unlimited degree of autonomy, choice, responsibility, and self-accountability.
3. Be alert to crises in the life of the young person. If there are particularly stressful times at school, with friendships, or in extracurricular activities, be available to talk over these problems. Provide the person with support and encouragement.
4. Teach the basics of good nutrition and exercise at home and in school.
5. Be careful when encouraging a young person to lose weight. Communicate that you love and care about the adolescent, regardless of how much he or she weighs, and that your concern is for the person's health and well-being.
6. If the person wants to begin a diet, find out why. If he or she feels inadequate and unaccepted, seek professional help from a therapist, psychologist, or mental clinic.
7. When weight loss is called for, the diet should be supervised by a physician. It should include a

physical examination, a set weight goal which will be adhered to, and a specific plan for losing the weight. The person should also be prepared to shift from a weight loss to a weight maintenance diet when the goal has been reached.

If you would like more information on A.N.A.D. and the groups, you are encouraged to write: A.N.A.D., Box 271, Highland Park, IL 60035.

There are so many reasons for going into such behavior as anorexia and bulimia. Putting the emotional aspects aside for a minute, here are some very tangible and key expressions and situations that come to mind. These messages come from various women's childhoods and play on those annoying tapes that cannot be erased, but can be understood and put into perspective while creating a new tape:

1. "Clean up your plate."
2. "Children are starving in other countries."
3. Constant fighting at the dinner table, and choosing to air the day's dirty laundry at the table.
4. Pressure from society to be thin and thus acceptable.

Try to take the individual's problems very seriously if at all possible. Try to understand the hills as they loom ahead of your son or daughter. Remember back to your own childhood for better insight into others' feelings of inadequacy and confusion. Recall how crushing it was to be rejected by one of your peers. You understand that life goes on, the sun always comes up the next morning, but to a young person in the middle of a crisis, there is no tomorrow, only today's devastation. The feeling of hopelessness when a steady broke up with you, a best friend turned her back on you, or the dread of coming home with an

"F" on a report card. There was no place to hide, no place to go except the one place on earth you didn't want to go—home. There were times when I felt like I could never again face my parents, and yet, I wanted to crawl up in their laps. I wanted to be an adult with an adult's perspective, but I wasn't; and I didn't have an adult's advantage of years of experience to draw from.

Remember the desolation and loneliness of having to move from one school to another, or going away to college without a friend awaiting you? Remember the disorientation and fear of the unknown?

Remember how it was to come home from school upset by a situation, only to feel like your problems were not important because Mom and Dad had been working all day and deserved to have problems, but you didn't, because all you did was go to school?

Remember all the physical changes taking place in your body at the time? The terrible confusion, the leg aches from growing, or how critical it was to belong to a group, the *right* group? The pain of not knowing as yet your place in the world, or how you were going to find it? Having to go to school, no sense of control over a body or a mind that seemed, for all intents and purposes, to be human—just a smaller version. Not being in the position to make any major decisions on your own; always at someone's beck and call, and always waiting for someone else to make decisions for you? Wanting desperately to be loved and to fit in? Remember? Perhaps feeling that no one cared, only wanted you to stay out of the way?

I'm not trying to put blame on parents, nor am I trying to make childhood sound like one big pity party. But when we can't communicate these feelings to the people we love, a deep volcano begins to fill with very painful feelings of anger, resentment, depression, confusion, frustration, anxiety, and inadequacy, often resulting in isolation, anorexia, or bulimia.

I often ask parents and spouses as well as friends of victims to put themselves in the other's place and try to feel what that person is experiencing before passing judgment or giving an opinion on what they don't feel qualified to evaluate. Give yourself a chance to help and share by comparing an experience with that of the victim. Try to find a common ground on which to relate and communicate. Perhaps in the sharing and relating, you can go one step further, and offer trust. It's wonderful when you can learn to educate yourself to trust and believe in the person. Hard? Not any harder than trying to help the life of a very rebellious and disturbed boy or girl.

A family forum is really helpful to families who find communication difficult. People's personalities differ, and so do attitudes, approaches to humor, and stress levels.

Ron and I counseled a family who didn't even attach the same meanings to the words they were using. The teenager said, "You're always pushy. I don't want to go to college, so quit pushing me toward it!"

The parents were completely confused. Their daughter had expressed the desire to become a doctor since she was small, because she wanted to! But suddenly their encouragement was inappropriate.

We suggested the daughter define "pushy" to her parents. "Pushy" meant holding the daughter's expectations and dreams as their own, because the dreams then became demands. To release their daughter to do her own dreaming would allow her to choose and fail without disappointing her parents.

The parents defined "encouragement" as wanting her to know she had their support, and that they wanted her to succeed. This led both sides to define "success." The girl defined it as doing what made her happy; the parents, as enough money to insure her future in the world.

All parties must be willing to redefine their words to themselves and their families. Understand what you are asking of one another and yourself during a family forum.

I always suggest that families meet once a week to talk about situations in the home that are uncomfortable for them. Carry a journal and be willing to jot down something about the awkward times when they occur. A forum is not meant to be a gripe session, although sometimes it turns into one. If possible, it should be more of an airing of the prior week, than an exposing of feelings usually kept under wraps until they are explosions.

Remember, everyone wins and no one loses. The idea is to understand better what makes the others and yourself tick.

If you bring anger to the forum, look at it for a couple of days to monitor your reaction. Write down when the anger occurred, and bring it to forum at another time. Get the others' reaction to your feelings about anger and what had taken place—with an open mind instead of an open wound.

Prepare before the forum; do your homework! Redefine your words, giving your real meanings, your real feelings. Go prepared to learn about yourself and your family.

I cannot give a glowing report for the family mentioned above. We are still working with them; and they are still struggling to get past their defensiveness with each other. But peace will come because they want it to.

Now let me speak to husbands for just a minute. For many of my young women, the worst days of the week are the weekends. A bulimic woman seems to appreciate it when the weekends are somewhat structured and planned. But the women I see do not like to approach what are supposed to be fun days without knowing what that fun is going to be. I realize it seems somewhat of a paradox, as for every other day they appear very much to want control; however, not on weekends.

I know, for myself, I still can't stand for a weekend to sneak up on me without knowing what Ron is thinking of for us to do at least part of the time.

If that is an imposition or an unrealistic request, then perhaps it could at least be brought up for discussion. Maybe the husband could decide on activities one week and the wife the next.

So many still have no idea why they binge every week. It is a total frustration to them until we begin going over exactly what they do on these days off.

"Usually, nothing. . . . I can't stand it!" Or, "My husband always asks me what I want to do, and he waits until Saturday morning to do it! Instantly I'm upset, and want to binge."

It seems incongruous to the husband who states, "If I don't consult her about things, she is angry and upset with me, so I try to let her make the plans." Or, "I just don't like to plan the weekend, I let it happen."

Please discuss this to see if a lack of communication is the culprit, and if a compromise can be arrived at to everyone's mutual satisfaction.

Allow me to end this chapter of self-help groups and concerned family and friends' participation by presenting a few Bible verses that can beautifully apply and offer comfort:

"Admit your faults to one another and pray for each other so that you may be healed" (James 5:16).

"Two can accomplish more than twice as much as one, for the results can be much better. If one fails, the other pulls him up, but if a man falls when he is

141

alone, he is in trouble" (Ecclesiastes 4:9-12).

"Also, on a cold night, two under the same blanket gain warmth from each other, but how can one be warm alone? And one standing alone can be attacked and defeated, but two can stand back-to-back and conquer; three is even better, for a triple-braided cord is not easily broken" (Ecclesiastes 4:9-12).

"I also tell you this—if two of you agree down here on earth concerning anything you ask for, my Father in heaven will do it for you. For where two or three gather together because they are mine, I will be right there among them" (Matthew 18:19, 20).

EIGHTEEN
FEELING GOOD

Am I ever worthy?

In *The Living Bible* I read: Romans 3:10-12: "No one is good—no one in all the world is innocent. No one has ever really followed God's paths, or even truly wanted to. Every one has turned away; all have gone wrong. No one anywhere has kept on doing what is right; not one."

Romans 3:20-24: "Now do you see it? No one can ever be made right in God's sight by doing what the law commands. For the more we know of God's laws, the clearer it becomes that we aren't obeying them; his laws were only to make us see that we are sinners" (Romans 3:20-24).

"Then what can we boast about doing, to earn our salvation? Nothing at all. Why? Because our acquittal is not based on our good deeds; it is based on what Christ has done and our faith in him. So it is that we are saved by faith in Christ and not by the good things we do" (Romans 3:27-28).

I guess that answers my question once and for all! God allows me a sense of self-esteem when I am trying to please myself in a way that is pleasing to him. It is accomplishing something that enables me to feel happy and good about myself. This is not to be confused with self-worth. I will never be worthy enough to work my way to heaven, or work my way into the hearts of other people. But I can experience self-esteem through effort, and feel good about that effort.

I could really relate to esteem when going through a binge cycle without binging and purging. There was absolutely no esteem connected with binging and purging mindlessly; but I loved the effort I was putting forth to recover, and received a terrific sense of esteem. It felt so good to know the cycle was there, but I could still opt for another way. It is necessary to feel good, and to allow those feelings of esteem so that progress can be ongoing.

Allowing that sense of self-esteem to build within myself was like putting money into the bank and watching it grow with interest! The better I felt about my efforts, the more I continued those efforts. And why not, it's a wonderful feeling! It feels great to begin getting better by trying and learning.

At first I was very confused about esteem and worth. At the time, it seemed both had to be achieved, and both were rewards for my accomplishments. Now since achievement and looking for rewards from achieving had become "the bad guys" to me, I had to become more aware of what each meant.

In the beginning I didn't feel as if I had very much self-esteem. For me, achieving esteem alone didn't feel legitimate, and what I experienced instead was a state of selfishness and unworthiness. To develop the physical aptitude that enabled me to play a good tennis game was fun, and I liked myself while playing. I felt skilled because my movements on the court were practiced, and I had worked hard in the pursuit of my small measure of esteem. Yet somehow it was wrong to be enjoying tennis, and I didn't value my right to self-esteem if it was to benefit only me. I needed for it to be approved, validated, and judged, because others' esteem was somehow more valid. Others could have a good time and it was okay—they deserved it. They were worthy enough, but I never was.

My worth was being challenged by my fun and esteem. I felt judged and I always came up short. I would have to give up my precarious esteem and work even harder for self-worth through their approval.

How long could I continue with this confusing discomfort? And was there a workable balance between my esteem (which was derived from an activity that was fun), and my worth (that I was acceptable because I was working and serving others)? If there was, I was not understanding it. I tried to clear my mind and put the situation in better perspective.

What exactly brought self-worth? I felt worthy when I cleaned the house, but not happy. Happiness, fun, and esteem were synonymous to me. I could not create a balance between my achieved worth and my achieved esteem.

What a comfort and relief to realize that self-esteem is not only valid but necessary. Whether it be tennis, golf, knitting, painting, skydiving or needlepoint— we need to find ways to feel esteem for ourselves, by ourselves. I clean my house for myself and my family so that I can feel good about *me*.

There was a time when the house had to be absolutely immaculate every Sunday, because every Monday my brother-in-law would come over with his family. I never felt that he liked me; so the house had to shine because I knew that he did like cleanliness. I was asking him to like me because the house met with his approval. I felt great for about the first five minutes when he admired the house; but for the next several hours—I felt just as inadequate as ever. The house had earned his seal of approval, but I had not. I was not a broom or a shiny floor, and I needed to be liked just for myself. I did not achieve esteem from cleaning the house for my brother-in-law—only dishpan hands.

I can now play tennis or any other sport and feel esteem, a sense of accomplishment for my efforts, without having to apologize for that pleasure. I play for me and it feels good!

Determine for yourselves what gives you a sense of esteem and build on it. Learn to feel good about accomplishing and enjoying that accomplishment. All work and no play makes for some very unhappy people!

Allow yourselves to feel good about coming out of bulimia. It takes a lot of time and effort to gain ground while recovering, so don't sabotage yourselves by constantly waiting for the other shoe to fall. Enjoy your self-esteem by seeking out and developing skills that bring you pleasure, and by practicing and refining your own personal formula for getting better.

I don't ever again want to feel as though I have to be worthy of another's approval or fit in to earn that worth. I want to like me and allow others to like me—because of what's inside, not what I can achieve.

NINETEEN
ACCENT THE
POSITIVE

Many of my girls complain about negative qualities. "I hate it that I'm so messy! My home is always a mess and even my husband can't understand why it has to be a pigpen. I can't believe I'm such a slob!"

June: "I'm a terrible liar. Ask me anything and I'll agree to it; but also expect me to call back at the last possible moment and cancel out on you. I always lie!"

I could certainly relate to this one. Remember my confusion about getting out of tennis dates?

Jerri: "I am compulsively late. I don't care how careful I am, or how badly I want to be there, I'll be late. Everyone ends up mad at me, including me!"

Myrna: "I'm angry with everyone. I shout at my children for no reason; and I never know when I'm going to fly off the handle."

There was a time when I would kick the vacuum cleaner for not picking lint up off the carpet!

I ask all my girls to make a list of as many of the so-called negative qualities as they can come up with. Then write down the positive ones as well. Bulimic women are not very aware of positive qualities, but they can fill a telephone directory with all the traits they dislike in themselves.

Naturally, heading the top of June's negative list was lying. I was so frightened of not fitting in and being liked that I would agree to anything, knowing even as the yes was rolling from my tongue, that I wouldn't follow through.

I hated the responsibility of having to cancel, and if it were possible, I would forget the whole thing. Only fearing I would run into the commitment again would compel me to pick up the telephone and cancel. I did not enjoy lying, and did not consider myself a compulsive liar. I was afraid. Any commitment was a responsibility, and all responsibility was a control. We all know by now how I felt about control!

When first writing my own list, I found I actually enjoyed honesty once I stopped trying to fit in with everyone and the fear of control was removed. Of course, I hated the negative quality of constantly getting out of things—lying. It went against my very real and positive quality; which was honesty.

June was also terrified of commitment. The closer an event approached, the more panicky she became.

By delving into her list honestly, we discovered that she never allowed herself choices. When she realized she could say no, she also realized she could accept the invitations she chose.

Of course, we all have some responsibilities that are without choice. But there are also usually several different alternatives open to us.

People accepted "no" from June. Their response to her choice was up to them. She became diligent in her efforts to be honest and honestly weigh their feelings. In doing so, she found her "no" was accepted as her decision, her choice. People respected her more for being honest and making those choices instead of leading them up to the appointed time and then slamming the door in their faces!

Always arriving late made Jerri mad at herself all over again. "At the last minute I think of everything else I need to be doing, or could be doing, to stall. Even if I start early, and with the best intentions, I'll mess around until I'm late. It becomes important to have them waiting for me." When talking further, "I never have people's attention any other time than when I walk in late. I'm so unimportant, no one cares one way or the other about me. In a room full of people, I go unnoticed. But when I'm late, I'm definitely noticed, even if it's only in frustration and anger."

Jerri discovered she possessed a very positive quality—punctuality. She now loves being on time and they appreciate her consideration as to their feelings.

When Jerri decided she could work on being more assertive in a group by just being herself and allowing others to get to know her a little better, she found she much preferred this.

Myrna was afraid of her own temper. She felt she never knew when it would appear, nor how the anger would expose itself. She was ashamed of the temper her children were seeing in her. It frightened them, and hurt her.

Myrna and I had something in common. Neither one of us was aware of how little anger had ever been expressed before for the real reason. It's like the last straw that broke the camel's back. The anger would be shoved back into our volcano. Fearing exposure and thus rejection, we didn't want to experience it. It was allowed to fester in the volcano, building pressure until the pressure caused an eruption. Unfortunately, kicking the vacuum didn't really help the original anger. It was still there in the volcano, ready to build pressure and erupt again, but always at the wrong time, for the wrong reasons.

Unfortunately, I also yelled at my son at times for the wrong reasons. I was sure he would never reject me, and I was confident I could expose anger without suffering any permanent consequences. I took advantage of the undeniable fact that I was his mother.

Many of my girls tell me at first, "But I do get angry; it seems like I'm mad all the time. Even as a teenager I was constantly rebelling and making my parents furious. I didn't enjoy it, but I just couldn't help it."

When identified, the rebellion can sometimes be recognized as a hurt. In Myrna's case, she had been forced to be a mother to eight other brothers and sisters at an age when she should have been mothered. She married early, had a baby immediately, and was very much regretting mothering all over again. She was really very angry with her own absentee mother for leaving her with such responsibilities. But she didn't want to face the fact that she was mad at Mom. Myrna now sees her frequently, and doesn't want her to leave again. In Myrna's mind, exposing the original anger might cause Mom to desert her again. This was a possibility she couldn't face. When she could, she realized she was not afraid of an uncontrolled temper, but of losing her mother again.

The opposite of temper for Myrna? A very good-natured and calm spirit.

Many a time I binged over dishonesty or anger that had originated a week or more before. It was almost as if my mind did it on purpose to throw me off the track. After the binge, I would go over what happened for the last twenty-four hours or so, only to come up empty. I soon learned to go back farther if the situation called for it and the symptoms were still there.

Something always triggered a binge. The original

trigger could be allowed to fester and settle, but it was only building pressure for the next eruption. When I understood the original anger, I backed up and found a satisfactory alternative.

If you are tired of your full negative column, then write your own traits down and examine them a little more closely. You may be very surprised to discover that you are actually the opposite of these esteem-destroying traits. The very fact that you dislike them so much is a strong indication that you could actually be the opposite, just not realizing the positive side of your qualities. Dare to examine them carefully in order to uncover and understand the original reason for adopting the negative side of your traits, and cultivate the positives. As an example, I have written my own list compiled very early in my recovery. Compare my original list.

NEGATIVE

1. A quitter—afraid of commitments.
2. A liar—afraid of control. I'll say anything and bank on being able to get out of it later—just don't box me in!
3. Selfish—afraid of opening up, an inadequacy when giving of myself to others; not worthy enough, anyway.
4. Stagnant—confusion from bulimia, not knowing where to go or turn for help.
5. Messy—my mind was messy, and I couldn't clear it long enough to see another mess.
6. Lazy—depression causes you to feel lazy.

Here is my new list and what I confess as positive affirmations. Notice that they are in direct conflict with my earlier negative list.

POSITIVE

1. Tenacious
2. Honest (I try anyway)
3. Caring
4. Growing
5. Organized
6. Athletic

TWENTY
WHAT IF?

So much of the pain of bulimia is not being aware of *choices*. I don't care what advice someone offered me, my automatic response was, *I can't*. Why? I never allowed a choice to penetrate and become a possible solution to anything. I had no idea then that nearly every decision had at least three alternatives.

Controlling my weight was a *have to*. To go over the one hundred mark was a fate worse than death. Really? I didn't allow a choice where my favorite control was concerned.

I needed to sit down and write down all the alternatives, and then face the terrible what-ifs in order to get a more realistic perspective. "What will happen if I gain ten pounds? Will my credit cards be automatically taken away? Will my son refuse to let me buy him clothes anymore? Or worse, will the elusive 'they' withdraw my membership from the human race?"

An alternative could be a weight gain of twenty or thirty pounds. Now we're talking serious trouble! It's enough to encourage a trip to a restaurant to inhale half its menu! Would I have to buy a bigger size in clothes? Or, what if I visited my family at Christmas, and I'm the only blimp in an ancestry of thin and controlled saints? My worse what if yet, now they'll know what a pig I really am inside and out. Oh, really? What are they going to do, withhold the Christmas bathrobe that's in the wrong color anyway?

If these are oversimplifications, forgive me my flippancy and sarcasm. But I found most of my what ifs were not the real culprits, not the real threats. My boogie man was: Everyone will see me stark naked without a stitch of protection, without an ounce of self-control, a blubbering and gurgling mass of undiscipline, a slobbering, drooling failure not even to be pitied, only hated.

Was that truly my worst fear? My worst what if? No! My worst what if was that they wouldn't kick me out, but instead hound me night and day, call constantly, judge me every day and every night from then on. I simply couldn't take a constant reminder of their disappointment and disgust of me! I would then force myself deeper into that prison of performing, struggling to fake my rehabilitation and give up any precious identity I had gained by somehow fitting in. Now, that really did scare me!

I can well remember as a child (who am I kidding, add girl and woman), dreading that my dad would find something out, but dreading even more that he would then judge me defective forever. I would wear my deficiency like a soiled piece of clothing.

Dad never said that. In fact, I remember when he found his cigarette carton broken into and asked me three times if I had smoked one. Three times I denied taking one out and smoking it behind his back. I didn't want his judgment. When he told me he would call the police, because it meant the house had been broken into, I confessed! He was hurt that I hadn't been honest with him. I felt that hurt, but only in the form of more upcoming judgment. *Now I'll never hear the end of it. I'll forever be the liar, never be trusted again. Dirty. Guilty. Again.*

For several days Dad was quiet and very hurt. When he did speak to me again, it wasn't what I had been expecting.

"I don't want to distrust you. Don't ever lie to me again; I don't care that you smoked a cigarette, only that you didn't tell me the truth. I'm going to forget that it ever happened. I'll never speak of it again."

At the time I couldn't accept that. In my mind I was still the liar, still guilty. I would have to be more clever in my deceptiveness next time.

To this day, my dad has never brought up the incident, but I remembered it very vividly from that time on. That was my choice, I decided to stay guilty and strive to keep further indiscretions a more carefully guarded secret.

Let me say now, what I never said then, "Thank you, Dad, for forgiving and forgetting; for never bringing it up again." I only wish I could have done the same. At the time, my most dreaded what if was being caught. It happened. Not only was I caught taking the cigarettes, but in lying *three times*. But the boogie man didn't strip me of my dignity, didn't publicly whip me. Dad didn't have to embarrass me; I was embarrassed. He didn't have to hurt me; I did it for him. My choice. My decision. Mom and Dad automatically forgave me because they loved me and understood my growing pains. I wish I could have been more forgiving, more honest instead of withdrawing, crawling into myself and creating that volcano.

"What a tangled web we weave, when first we practice to deceive."

I chose to build that volcano, and I chose the very hot and uncomfortable feelings that were to one day cause the eruptions.

Ellie cries, "I have to go to my in-laws today, and I don't want to, but my husband is making me!"

First, who's making whom? Is there a gun at your head? Is God going to cause a truck to run over you if you don't? Will the in-laws converge on your home and carry you off into the bushes by the hair yelling and screaming?

What if she chose to stay home and not feel guilty about that choice. Only she can judge herself for not going. Only she can give them permission to judge her for not going. She can choose to tell them she's simply not up to a visit at this time, and then choose to be free of their imposed guilt. Perhaps they are afraid of her judgment and putting on an offensive front to protect themselves. Or, she could stay home and hate herself and them; or go and be miserable, hating them, her husband, and herself.

The point is, there are many more alternatives than we seem to see at the time, or allow ourselves to see. "I have to" usually does not exist.

What I have to do always meant, I have to eat everything first, then I have to make an appearance, be controlled. First, I have to allow a release if I can't allow the release that comes from making choices with others.

Ellie had called me with her dilemma before automatically going downstairs and consuming an entire cake. That was her way of dealing with the controlling situation. That way, she would have been making the choice to romp in the playpen first, then suffer by performing for her in-laws in order to fit in and be accepted. She decided to make another choice instead: calling me. Half an hour later, she didn't have to eat to face the responsibility of dealing with her options. A far better choice!

TWENTY-ONE
RECIPE FOR
SUCCESS

The physical as well as the emotional symptoms of bulimia have to be treated. I had to find ways to slow the binging just to feel strong enough to delve into the reasons for my illness.

While I couldn't bear to think about dieting in any form, I needed some esteem-producing successes to encourage myself to keep trying.

I am going to offer several of the more successful ideas that have worked for me and others. Try all of them; throw out the ones that don't work; and incorporate the ones that do into your formula.

First, I want to share a few experiences from my files that may help you understand what some binges are really saying. Sometimes, as you grow to understand, relaxation takes place automatically.

Rita looks at her stomach in the mirror the first thing every morning. She weighs ninety-five pounds, yet she often feels her stomach is terribly protruded when she is not happy with her ability to cope with her life and surroundings.

While trying to understand why her need to have a

flat stomach was so tied in with her feelings of inadequacy, she made a startling discovery.

"I wake up and dread getting out of bed in the morning because I know I'm going to look in the mirror at my stomach and hate it! The bulge is still there! Why can't I get rid of it? Just like responsibilities—they're always there; they never go away. I can't get rid of my stomach or my responsibilities; and I can't face either one!"

One of Gina's favorite binge foods is mashed potatoes. Gina is a long way from Mom and Dad. The only time she goes home is Christmas; and the holiday feast always means mashed potatoes.

"I didn't realize that many binges were because I was homesick. Gorging myself on mashed potatoes was my way of coping with missing my parents and home."

Iris experiences her bulimic cycles in the middle of the night. She needed to wake up enough to ask herself to feel what was going on before the binge. She discovered she had always been afraid of the dark. At home when she awoke at night, she would get into bed with Mom, where it was safe. Now Mom isn't there, but the refrigerator is. When she allowed herself to feel her fear of darkness, she could rationally deal with it. As an adult she was no longer afraid of the dark, but the child within was still listening to the tape that dictated the fear. She began letting the parent soothe the child, assuring her that everything was all right. Iris remembered that as a little girl she had been told that nighttime meant God was asleep. The sun was his eyelids opening up.

As an adult she knew that wasn't true, but first she had to face the remembrance and the feelings, then explain it to the little girl within herself. Relief!

I never binged without being very, very aware of an all-consuming hyper attitude. The more I ate, the faster my actions became. Everything in my mind was accelerated to a fever pitch. There was no calming down, until I was so stuffed, there was nothing left to feel but sickness and then exhaustion. The cycle was over.

Be very conscious of slowing down before eating, or even before being around food. Take deep breaths and try to eat very slowly, especially when not on a binge, in order to get into the habit of enjoying the taste of each mouthful, enjoying textures and smells. Put your fork down in between bites, consciously practicing and learning to respect food during the normal cycles.

I still do a good deal of walking when hyper. I slow the world down to my pace, watch the people, thank God for two legs to walk with and two eyes with which to marvel at nature in all its colors and smells. For a short time everything is marching to the beat of my drum, and I feel calm and tranquil—enough so that the tension is gone and I can relax.

Also, realize the healing will have to take place from the inside. It will eventually show on the outside, but for awhile try to be content with a slow healing. You may decide to try taking the responsibility for what goes into your stomach by not purging. If so, you may put on a little weight for awhile. I did, going up to 140 pounds. It wasn't fun, but I was determined to put aside my anxiety about weight and concentrate on what I was learning from the inside. When I knew I was going to keep on the binges, they began to taper. It took what seemed a lifetime to me, but the binges turned into just sporadic overeating, and then more normal habits. My weight metabolized, and I then began to lose again. It didn't happen overnight—but I hadn't gotten bulimia overnight.

When eating with people, be very conscious of tuning them in, and the food out.

I'll never forget an experience I had with an acquaintance of mine. I knew I was uncomfortable around her, but had no idea to what extent, until one day I was sitting in her kitchen, watching her prepare a light lunch for the two of us. I was listening to her until she launched on to a subject that caused me to feel trapped and defensive.

All of a sudden, I became terribly aware of a chocolate cake sitting on her table to the side of me. I was looking right at her, and not hearing a word she said!

She left the room, and I attacked her cake! I couldn't believe myself. When she came back, I blamed her dog (he was huge and she was used to having him help himself).

Then it hit me! I had tuned her out and the food in, because I was threatened and uncomfortable in my inability to cope. With this realization came understanding, and with understanding came an idea. If I could tune food in, then I could also tune it out! I started concentrating on what she was saying, consciously tuning her back in and the cake out. It worked!

Experiment with this idea; if I can do it, you can too.

I needed to find my trigger areas—what situations seemed to initiate a binge. For me it was dishonesty. Anytime I was deliberately not being honest with myself about my feelings, I would binge. I had to become very aware of what my true feelings were.

If I had been more aware of them when the uncomfortable conversation and the cake caper were about to occur, I could have let my acquaintance in on my discomfort. Perhaps I could have asked her to not discuss the threatening subject. I might not have liked her reaction and spent a few miserable minutes, but in the long run, it would have been worth it.

I had to learn to find alternatives to situations other than binging. Ironic, but even an excess five pounds could mean a binge rather than watching my weight for a couple of weeks. My decision not to accept the responsibility of losing weight would cause me to choose the irresponsibility of mindlessly binging, and then the quick way out of that irresponsibility—purging.

Now for diet tips, bulimic style:

1. Know what you are going to do upon finishing a meal. Try to stick to it. Push the food away and do whatever you have planned.
2. When cleaning up after a meal, remember, unusable remains of meals belong in mechanical food disposals, not your mouth!
3. Fantasize more about a well future. Create images in your mind and try to see that they come true. Perhaps imagine a place in your mind to go to when you are tense. Stay there until the feeling passes.
4. Change patterns. If you feel antsy at 3 o'clock in the afternoon, then, if possible, plan a walk or other relaxing activity for that time.
5. Rehearse a well-known pressure situation. If you know a certain event or person is always going to threaten you, perhaps you can prepare for that circumstance and then cope, as opposed to always reacting negatively or always going on a binge.
6. Try to introduce some binge food items into your diet at a time other than when binging. Take the forbidden fruit aspect out of it. I began having a piece of cake or pie after a normal meal or when I was not interested in binging. I didn't gain weight from one piece of anything and it didn't automatically force a binge.

7. Watch normally thin people eat. Notice how careful they are not to get too full. They are afraid of a full feeling the way we are afraid of an empty one! I remember watching a woman at a pie shop. She ordered a salad and a piece of pie at the same time, then proceeded to eat the pie first. The sweet treat was the reason she had come, and she ate it first because she knew she would get full, and wouldn't be able to eat all of the salad. On the other hand, I had already consumed an entire head of lettuce because I was afraid I wouldn't get full enough to be hungry for the whole pie!

2:11: "Just as my mouth can taste good food, so my mind tastes truth when I hear it." Job 13:5: "Oh, please be quiet! That would be your highest wisdom."

Be more open to hear what your child within is trying to say; and be very careful not to judge her or ask her to feel stupid. *Listen.*

These last pages are additional diet tips that really helped me to understand that poor mistreated and misunderstood organ in the middle of my body. I hope they will be able to help you too.

1. Eat a meal or snack only after you have asked yourself, "Why?" "What need am I satisfying by eating?" If I am eating only for the gratification of the stomach, then I had better be sure the stomach is really hungry. The brain knows no end to its gratification. It is never full, never without the desire for more. It knows only to expand its capacity to grow, whether it be in information or wisdom. This is good, as you never want it to be too full of ideas or understanding. But realize that because it never wants to quit, it must not be allowed full reign in areas that do not fall under its domain. Such areas include food, drink, and drugs. It can

rule only your mental powers. The stomach's domain is the hunger it needs in order to perpetuate the brain's fulfillment of its duties, and to keep the body in good physical condition. It's a machine to keep you alive, a ticket to long life through proper care of yourself. Allow your brain and your stomach to function independently. They should come in contact with one another only when the stomach signals the brain that it needs food, and when it subsequently triggers the full mechanism in the brain. Then both organs function together happily and smoothly, in harmony and mutual cooperation.

2. Now that you have them working in their proper place, turn off anxiety, fear, dread, insecurity, and doubt. These are negative forms of destruction that serve only as fuel for a confused brain. They are parasites to your effectiveness and must be turned off. Do it with a sense of accomplishment. It's like having a weight lifted off your mind.

3. Always prepare before you eat, and always sit down to eat. Are you hungry? Ask your stomach. Do you need nourishment at this time in order to sustain creativity or activity? Ask your stomach. Remember, you have a normal appetite for food, but a large appetite for fun and creativity!

4. Excess feeding of the stomach is not a religious experience. It will not bring you one bit closer to happiness, but only serve to make you more unhappy. Stay in touch with your stomach, and when it starts to let you know it is almost full, begin thinking of all the things you want to accomplish right then. Pick up a book, leave the room, get a glass of water, or begin daydreaming. Anything to stop the nervous gesture of lifting the fork to the mouth again and again.

5. Always be consciously clearing your mind, cleansing it with questions. Are there any unsolved

problems that could cause a mental problem or stumblingblock now or later?

6. Food should be prettily arranged. Eat it slowly. Don't attack it! Relish its smell and taste. Take time to value it as something delicate and pleasing. Don't kill it as you would like to kill your hidden emotions. You can't destroy food as it gets in your way—it will only be there next time. Respect food; don't hate it!

7. When you awake in the morning, visualize yourself eating three normal meals. See yourself so full after dinner, you wouldn't possibly be able to eat another thing.

8. If you should slip, remember to continue with your positive thinking. You will gain from every slippage because you are recovering more and more, and you're never going to be perfect.

9. Remember, no one is going to take your independence away from you. Only you can do that. Others can suggest and advise, but the ultimate decision is always yours. No one can take anything away from you without your permission. You are unique; no one else will ever be quite like you. That is the way God meant it to be. He loves you for your uniqueness.

TWENTY-TWO
IN THE
BEGINNING

Ron and I had a "junk" room. We endured its existence for one year. In that year, the door was always kept closed. Every time I passed it, I cringed a little. Every time I bypassed it, while cleaning the rest of the house, I cringed a little more. No matter how hard I tried, I couldn't forget that a thin partition of wood was all that separated me from junk, dirt, and things that go bump in the night. Ignoring it became difficult; and soon it was impossible to forget that room was there. Avoiding the inevitable clean up was simply no longer possible! It was patronizing to try to convince myself that tackling the junk room would afford me about thirty days of healthy exercise!

So I pacified and tempted myself with visions of enjoying spring through the windows of a sunny sewing room. (Dreaming is less patronizing, don't you think?) I pictured bright yellow curtains adorning the windows, a soft and comfortable flower-speckled armchair, ever ready to coax weary but faithful family members into watching me sew.

With visions of yellow material floating in my head,

I grabbed scrub brush and pail, broom and ladder, and cans of cleanser.

Gingerly grasping the knob to the entrance meant victory—but also holding my breath in dread of something flying out to grab me. I peeked in.

Well, at least I'm still in one piece, and thankfully nothing is jammed against the door. I'm sure that's a good sign . . . isn't it?

Naturally, the window hadn't as much as been cracked open the whole year. I had thought the first of my senses to be offended would be my eyes; but I was wrong. It was my poor unprepared nose! Instead of the sweet fragrance of fresh air, I was assailed with the odor of dirty carpet that had not been aired, only abused, for about twenty years. Thank goodness the roof didn't leak or I'd have been inhaling a moldy smell as well. I don't know what qualifies as a refuge for wildlife these days, but I'm sure my future sewing room was right in there for top consideration. It was a veritable paradise for all creatures large and small; a preserve complete with a stuffy climate control!

Now, I'm sure you're asking yourself, "Just what has airing Jackie's dirty laundry, or in this case her junk room, got to do with bulimia?"

It took a certain amount of courage to stay in that room after facing the awesome amount of work ahead of me; it was not a pretty sight. But anything worth having is worth working for. I wanted that sewing room and was willing to put the effort into having it. Goodness knows, it had to be done. So the assumption of responsibility had to fall, for the most part, on my shoulders alone. It would have seemed easier to have thrown up my hands, go running from the room, and lock it again behind me. But since no one else really knew exactly how I wanted my sewing room to look, my family had already dealt with the "trying to please Jackie" syndrome a few thousand times before. Now I had to take the bull by the horns myself.

I decided to divide the work load into days. First I'd come up with a plan for what I was going to do; and then a schedule to help me determine when I would do it. My first step was to move everything out so that I could see more objectively what would be needed to get the job done. The next day, after everything was out of the room, I started cleaning the cobwebs from the ceiling. Then I began on the ceiling itself. Notice . . . not the carpet, not the walls or the windows—just the cobwebs and the ceiling. Otherwise, I couldn't have determined whether the walls needed to be repainted, or just washed.

I could accept what was ahead of me only if I allowed myself room to organize, set up a schedule, and take one section of the plan at a time. I could not push myself to have a thoroughly clean, immaculate, and creative sewing room by 5 o'clock that evening!

Now, let's get back to overcoming bulimia, or any other task that seems insurmountable. Yes, there is an awesome amount of work ahead of you in order to recover, and I have no intention of minimizing it for you. But remember, anything worth having is worth putting the time and effort into. But always with the proper preparation.

You might as well ask that all-important question, "Do I really want to give up my eating disorder? And if I do, what will I have to take its place?" Ask it now, before even contemplating opening the door to your own junk room. I had to give a resounding "yes" before I could ever begin recovery. Whatever the future holds, it has to be better, because it will be honest. I simply couldn't live the lie of my existence any longer. You, too, must make the same decision. As far as replacing bulimia—once you have begun the cleanup, you'll find self-esteem comes from ac-tivities that help you feel good about yourself. Re-covering from bulimia will definitely help you to feel good about yourself. Remember, there is no esteem in shoving your head into a toilet! Discovering other ways to fill the voids in your life are self-esteem builders, as well as just time fillers. Dare to take the chance!

Now, open the door to your mind and be willing to look at the entire picture; then divide the work load into sections as I have done in previous chapters. Your own personal formulas will probably vary, so experiment until it fits *you*. Make sure you are allow-ing time to breathe between cleaning sessions. Re-assess your progress after each step has been initiated, delved into, or at least given an honest appraisal. Allow a chance to learn, to grow. Allow time to step back a few paces to view an area that is still in need of attention before continuing.

Be willing to clean the cobwebs first. Look at the early symptoms of bulimia: isolation, depression, and others you are experiencing. Don't demand of yourself that binging and purging be stopped im-mediately! Do not set yourself up for that kind of pressure! I did not demand anything of myself, ex-cept that I be as honest as possible in my motives and my deeds. Patience is a very important part of re-covery. Stay as true to your plan as possible. Take one step at a time. Otherwise the cobwebs of the symptoms will form again and fall upon the floor of your good intentions. Going ahead of yourself might even cause you to feel you have to start all over again due to guilt and discouragement. The cobwebs are going to have to be looked at from time to time anyway, but there's no point in doing unnecessary damage or work before you're ready.

Next step? Cleaning the cobwebs only uncovers

walls in dire need of attention. Now, dare to look at the walls of your identity (or lack of it). Go back into your memory to find out when the dishonesty (arising out of a need to protect yourself) began. Look at the ways and means you devised to perpetuate that false security. Facing the binging symptoms first, zero into when you began building the volcano to hide from the early symptoms. Can the walls be washed? Is the understanding of why the symptoms arose in the first place enough? Or will the walls have to be repainted by creating more affirmative tapes? Only you can determine the amount of cleaning necessary.

Rome was not built in a day. I did not clean the room in a day. I did not recover in a day. I began with a plan and insight into a personal formula that I have tried to give to you. Do not go ahead of yourself or allow undue expectations that will only serve to drag you down.

Overcoming bulimia is a challenge, perhaps the greatest one you'll ever face, because through it will come the revealing of your own identity, and of your relationship with God.

When cleaning your walls, be honest in coping and dealing with your life. Cleaning always leads to more cleaning; that is part of the challenge of recovery. I am never through growing, never through recovering, never through cleaning my house within. I am no longer afraid of soap and water, only of a room deodorizer—designed to cover up!

Let me give you another example of cleaning that house you live in by taking one step at a time. When *Confessions of a Closet Eater* was first conceived, I had no idea when or how the book would become a reality. On my own, I floundered and couldn't seem to get started. But my editors made the task just as flexible as possible. It was that flexibility that enabled me to reassess what I wanted to write; yet it didn't intimidate me so I couldn't begin.

As long as I was insisting on writing an entire book from cover to cover in thirty days, I was in deep, deep trouble. The awesome responsibility of such an undertaking was more than I could face. My publisher released me from any paralysis and my inability to cope, with one short sentence, "We want one chapter at a time. First a beginning, then a middle, and finally an end."

Wow! It was like putting salve on an open wound. One chapter at a time. One step at a time! All in God's good timing and on God's time schedule. I went home on clouds of relief.

Everything in my life can be divided into sections; and in Christ I will be able to handle one section at a time. I determined to understand one phase of my personality at a time, one step at a time.

When bringing several chapters to my publisher one day, Ron and I stopped off at a beautiful restaurant for lunch. It was about 3 o'clock in the afternoon. Usually, by that time, I have already eaten and am halfway into my afternoon. I was antsy, tense, hungry, feeling bulimic! As we were shown to our table, I sat there mentally and physically coiled to kill, or at least to erupt all over the place. All the while, and without realizing my feelings, Ron was busy admiring the lovely pond wth fish that flowed through the area. I sat there in an absolute tizzy, furious with Ron because he wasn't feeling the same tension I was. I watched others being shown to their tables and couldn't believe how stable they appeared as they would stop before the pond and draw one another's attention to it. I wondered how they could bear just to stand there and not rush to their tables for that life-giving substance—food!

Then it hit me! Every now and then I forget that I

am still bulimic. Those of us who have it are different, and I don't know if we will ever completely change. But, I do get hungry! And my hunger does cause me to get hyper if I wait too long to eat.

I also am aware that certain tests have been conducted on so-called "normal" people, and then on those with eating disorders. Our highs were much higher, and our lows were much lower. I don't know about you, but that makes me feel a lot better.

Upon recognizing this, I could look at those people, and even Ron, and tell myself I wanted and needed food. I get hungry; and when I don't eat within a time frame I am used to, I become hyper. It isn't just a matter of still clinging to a residue of bulimia; nor do I fear charging back into the symptoms. The simple fact is, *I am different.* Everyone with an eating disorder is a little different from the norm. This understanding means I can sit back, relax, look at the waiter and say, "Bring me a roll, and please bring it now." I no longer have to eat the whole basket of bread to soothe some hidden and unknown secret inside. I just need a roll, or whatever, to calm myself down a little. Then I, too, get to admire the pond, the fish, my husband, even my food.

Vive la difference! I know, *easy for me to say.* Take heart; you'll be able to say that, too. *That* difference has made me a much happier person, because I learned my own formula to a more complete relationship with myself, my loved ones, and my God.

I have many people ask me, "Why can't God just change me? Why can't he just take these awful symptoms away?"

When Angie's boy was a baby, he refused to become potty trained. No matter how she tried to persuade him to use the bathroom, he wouldn't. There was absolutely no reason for him to do so. Every time

he even looked like he was going to wet his diaper,
Angie was there to change and powder him so quickly, he had no idea what discomfort was. Naturally,
he didn't want to have learn to go to the bathroom;
there was no need, he wasn't uncomfortable!

She left him with her mother one day, and in the
evening retrieved a little boy no longer sporting a
diaper and rubber pants. Mom didn't feel like running
around behind him with a washcloth, baby powder,
and a disposable. She had the unmitigated gall to let
her daughter's pride and joy slosh around until he
decided that his Grandma wasn't going to fix his
predicament. She parked his little fanny on the toilet
and told him of both their responsibilities. His was to
use the toilet, and hers was to help him. By now,
bright red from his discomfort, he promptly accepted
his responsibility, took her word that he would automatically feel better, and—voila!—one potty-trained
and very relieved little boy—and mother.

As a bulimic woman I, like many others, had asked
God to change me because I was uncomfortable. But,
like Angie's boy, I had to feel the wetness long enough,
be uncomfortable enough, to—first feel the *wet,* determine that I *wanted* to be changed, and then decide
just how willing I was to accept the responsibility for
that change.

I wanted it, but on my terms. I wanted not to suffer
from the symptoms a moment longer. But I wasn't
willing to take the time to accept responsibility for
binging and purging. I had to stay uncomfortable
and continue to binge and purge, until I decided I had
been uncomfortable long enough. I kept reminding
God that he hadn't taken the bulimia away. Still he
left me until I was not only tired of the condition, but
ready to initiate the change. Ready to experience the
feelings I had been so carefully avoiding.

I learned I could go into depression and come out

on top, and all without binging and purging. I could be antsy and get over it without swallowing the feeling, cramming it into my volcano until there was no longer space even to breathe!

There's nothing wrong with negative feelings, nothing wrong with being uncomfortable—it's what you do with the *discomfort* that will make the difference.

I had endured five years of symptoms, and that was enough for me. I had had it! God was there waiting for me to decide I was ready to feel, and to accept the responsibility for my recovery through him.

That acceptance may be difficult if your concept of God is so formal and distant that you don't feel he is accessible. Even praying may be hard if you feel he is only available for emergencies, or too busy for a sinner such as yourself. God is as close to me as I want him to be. I choose to believe that he listens to every need, every desire I bring to him. I didn't always feel he was that attainable; for many years, I was not even close to allowing him into every part of my life.

Everywhere I turned I had heard, "Take it to God." I wanted to, but simply didn't know how! I kept envisioning him about a thousand steps away on this very slick, cold, marble stairway. By the time I had reached the top of those stairs and got into his holy presence, I would feel exhausted and burned out. He just seemed too far away, too inaccessible for me.

As long as God was way up there, and I was way down here, I was going to have a problem communicating with him at all. By calling Jesus my friend, I could visit him any time about anything. It became a terribly personal relationship, and one that was essential for my recovery.

Obviously, I am going to stumble and fall again, but that doesn't mean I should stop trying.

Overcoming bulimia is a job, and I made it my job to recover. I couldn't just ask for God's faith, and then leave him to do the work. I ask for my portion of faith each day, and then work hard in conjunction with that faith. It wasn't easy, and the three years seemed like a long time. But, believe me, it's worth it.

Notice that I have been very careful not to claim a cure. To do so would be to claim that I never fail. I have not binged or purged for at least five years, but I don't have any claim or guarantee. I live my recovery every day and so can you. Please do not get me wrong. I am not suggesting that every day is a struggle; such is not the case. However, there are times when, if enough dishonesty with myself exists and is prolonged, I am hungry beyond my normal appetite. Bulimia is like a bright red light that goes on at such times, indicating that a problem exists. I then, after first appeasing myself with maybe a dessert or sandwich (quite a difference from the 40,000-calorie appeasements of the past), try to figure out the dishonesty. Then the exaggerated hunger goes away, and the problem is corrected. No one's life is perfect; no one's life is without trial. Growth is on-going and never complete.

At this time I would like to acknowledge my gratitude and love to my husband, Ron, and my son, Jeff. They stood by me through thick and thin, and I pray I will be able to do the same for them whenever they need, or just want me. They never judged me, although I'm sure there were times when they wanted to wring my neck! I love you, Ron. I love you, Jeff. You are forever my boys.

Let me also give thanks to my mom, my friend, who even came to baby-sit for her little girl when the symptoms were such that I really wanted and needed her. When I didn't think I could make it, she never doubted that I could, and never hesitated to tell me so. She never even questioned my ability to overcome my affliction, my trial. She hurt when I hurt, and bandaged my wounds with her comfort and wonderful mother's love. I love you, Mom.

And Dad—I could tell him I had just burned his house down, and he would find an acceptable excuse and reason for the burning. What do you say about someone who just loves you no matter what your faults or shortcomings are? He is there, just a phone call away, with all the right things to say. Thank you, Dad, for being you, and for being my dad—I love you.

My brother, Mike, was the highlight of my childhood. I mothered him as much as he would let me, and loved every minute of it. He remains my friend today, and my confidant whenever I need him. Only now, we mother one another. I love, you Mike.

Psalm 116:1:
I love the Lord because he hears my prayers and answers them. Because he bends down and listens, I will pray as long as I breathe!

Death stared me in the face—I was frightened and sad. Then I cried, "Lord, save me!" How kind he is! How good he is! So merciful, this God of ours! The Lord protects the simple and the childlike; I was facing death and then he saved me. . . . He has saved me from death, my eyes from tears, my feet from stumbling. I shall live! Yes, in his presence—here on earth! In my discouragement I thought, "They are lying when they say I will recover." But now what can I offer Jehovah for all he has done for me? I will bring him an offering of wine and praise his name for saving me. I will publicly bring him the sacrifice I vowed I would. His loved ones are very precious to him and he does not lightly let them die.

O Lord, you have freed me from my bonds and I will serve you forever. I will worship you and offer you a sacrifice of thanksgiving. Here in the courts of the Temple in Jerusalem, before all the people, I will pay everything I vowed to the Lord. Praise the Lord.

Just when I think the pain is over,
  And I pray I've found the key,
I confess my awareness is growing—
  And I fear the hidden "me."
Just when I vow—I'll love "her";
  And armed with my faith—turn the key.
My confessions turn to slander—
  And I fear the hidden "me."
Why, when "we" merge more and more—
  Do I feel like a fraud and a fake!
I pray to relax the rigidity,
  But when I slip—I can feel my heart break.
Someday I'll learn to accept "her."
  Someday she'll learn to "let go."
I want to get well, but I'm frightened.
  It's so hard to "reap what I sow."
Just when I think the pain is over,
  And I pray I've found the key,
I confess my awareness is growing—
  And I'll accept—the hidden "me."

GET WELL CARDS

To get better, I had to get in touch with the emotions that were continually erupting from my volcano. Because their exposure had meant discomfort as a child, it frightened me to risk that same exposure as an adult. I saw how others seemed to express feelings, and I also saw what happened when these feelings got out of control. Crying endlessly, beating children, getting angry beyond reason—would I become like that? I had devoted so much time and energy to hiding from them; would they now destroy me?

I took a deep breath and decided to take it one step at a time. First, I had to identify the feelings, one at a time. Surely that wouldn't hurt me. I latched onto the dictionary, and started looking up meanings. Each feeling got the benefit of one card. The definition, how I felt I had been avoiding it; how I could express it now without doing harm to myself or someone else. Always with the objective of rehearsing the exposure, so that I wouldn't have to be so frightened when it happened.

I had to see the questions before I could choose to be responsible for the answers.

I made a new card every week and worked on only one emotion at a time, always being very careful to concentrate on that card.

I started off all the people I counsel in this same way. My cards are called homework, and are given once a week. It is an important step to recovery.

As the weeks pass and you become habitual in their usage, the binging tapers off. If you can, try to think of bulimia as being like an algebra problem. You can see the solution any time you want: simply never binge or purge again. However, in order to arrive at the solution permanently, you have to learn to work your way through the problem, or learn the formula. My cards helped me learn the formula.

It's as if I had been at the bottom of a mountain and was now beginning the ascent to the top. The cards helped me get there. When I crested, I was aware of all the future trials in my life in the form of hills; but because I already had the formula for the climb, the hills are much smaller than the mountain.

The first card is a simple lesson in assertive training. The object is to start saying affirmatives, even though you may not believe them, instead of constantly listening to all the negatives in your head. It is especially helpful to say them before, during, and just after a binge. Memorize them right away, and repeat them at least three times a day. Even when much better, remain faithful to their affirmations.

Notice how the card reads. Realize it will take time for you to register and believe the new tape. Be patient, realistic, and consistent. Commit yourself to completing one card a week, not going on to the next until you thoroughly understand the previous one. Be careful not to judge your progress or someone else's by the answers. Everyone is different and views his or her feelings differently.

Card No. 1/Affirmations

1. I believe in myself and my ability to get well.
2. I now make the commitment to understand my emotions, and I look forward to breaking the destructive and manipulative pattern of these emotions.
3. I want to know myself in every sense, and I am eager to fulfill this commitment to myself.
4. I realize that only when I face these emotions will I get well.
5. Only the truth will set me free.

Say these truths before binging or purging—don't try to stop the binge yet. Just think about the new tape being turned on and playing the proper feedback, with no guilt! Realize it will take time for you to register and believe the new tape. Give yourself time!

The intent of Card 2 will be to help you gain a more honest appraisal of your present course in life. It's difficult to feel motivation for the now, as well as for a new future, if you don't know where you have been or were going. Don't put the past behind you, or kick out the previously charted future until you're better able to understand why it can no longer carry you to your new destination—a successful recovery.

Let's look at No. 2. It will involve sorting realistic goals from unrealistic. First ask yourself the questions that I did (pp. 182, 183). Then make three separate lists from the realistic point of view: More realistic; Realistic; and Goals for the near future. (See pp. 183, 184.) It's vital to have a direction for the day. It doesn't matter if you only commit yourself to "Today, I wash my hair and brush my teeth"; make sure the list is completed by the end of the day. It's wonderful to know that you are capable of accomplishing what you set out to do. Hopefully, it will encourage you to eliminate goals and objectives that are unrealistic and esteem destroying.

If I am looking out my office window and notice it is dirty, I have two choices at that time. I can feel terrible because I have no intention of washing it now (thus I am a sloppy housekeeper); or I can opt to put, "Wash office window Tuesday," on my next week's goal card and feel organized. This is good because I'm not forcing myself to do something that I don't have the time or the inclination and self-esteem to do. That's productive, that's recovery, and I feel better about the future.

If I want to become a brain surgeon, I write that on my Future Goal list. I don't write, "Worry about becoming a surgeon" on my *today* goal list. If I want to put, "Today, I take a course in surgery," great! That's productive, that's moving positively toward my future goal. But I don't want to worry about something that I'm not prepared to do anything about today. That would cause anxiety and pressure, and I would feel I was on my way to failure. There is no esteem in that kind of fuzzy thinking.

Let's try to remove unrealistic expectation's from yourself and others. Be more aware of what you are capable and desirous of expecting now, and in the future. Be aware of what you expected of yourself as a child and how it has changed. It will help you evaluate where the esteem rose or dropped, and why.

Cut down as much as possible on the *I should's,* and home in on *I want.* "I want to clean that office window next Tuesday. I'll feel better about myself." Not, "I have to clean it right now or judge myself worthless." You might want to jot down every time you say to yourself, *I should.* I counted twenty should's one time before my head ever left my pillow. It was enough to make me stay in bed!

When I first developed Card 2, these were my original answers. They will help guide you as to the absolute need to be honest with yourself. Fill it out quickly, then wait a few days while you think about it, and answer again. I think you'll be as surprised as I was!

What do I expect of myself?
1. To grow in Christ
2. To lose weight
3. Keep a clean house
4. Die
5. Stop hiding
6. Be honest
7. Be a good mother
8. Be the center of the family
9. Know what I want to be

What do I expect of others?
1. To throw me away, reject me
2. Uncover my deceptions and corruptions
3. Take my self-respect and not give it back
4. Use me
5. Like me as long as I play up to them
6. Not like the real me

182

What do I expect of loved ones?
1. Let me throw temper tantrums and understand
2. Always turn the other cheek
3. Let me deceive them
4. Always guess what I want, when I want it
5. Walk on eggs around me
6. Always be available
7. Always be strong individuals
8. Try to please me

Unrealistic
1. Have beautiful, long, flowing hair
2. Always be very thin
3. Have a "daddy-daughter" relationship
4. See every trial as a challenge
5. Never lie or be dishonest again
6. Be financially able to surprise my loved ones with extravagant gifts
7. Have Mom live with me
8. Feel more feminine
9. Never be selfish again
10. Always seek God's plan for my life
11. Succeed at everything
12. Never get hurt again
13. Live forever

More realistic list
1. Be all things to all people and fail
2. Fit in everywhere I go
3. Lie and be dishonest
4. Get lost with given directions
5. Fail at anything new
6. Always fight my weight
7. Be depressed
8. Never find my pot of gold
9. Never be happy
10. Fail, be embarrassed, and lose

Realistic goals
1. Push food away, accept that I am full
2. Go the whole day not worrying about my next "fix"
3. Find activities and hobbies to really make me happy
4. Insist I have fun
5. Try new things without fear of failure
6. Seek the Lord's guidance more

7. Look forward to going to church and Sunday school
8. Have family activities centered around the church
9. Be with people of my choice
10. Face challenges, not run
11. Not eat until I'm full
12. Own a women's center for all women-related feelings
13. Write my book on bulimia
14. Have a happy sex partner
15. Don't feel so controlled when touched
16. Complete daily list

Goals for near future
1. Think about book
2. Give more control to God
3. Open own bank account
4. See results for women
5. Enjoy church as a family
6. Lose five pounds
7. Be faithful to cards
8. Stay close to Mike
9. Be more aware of family's feelings

Card No. 2/Expectations

1. What do I expect of myself? (Be specific; my
   first list was not.)
2. What do I expect of others?
3. My goals—all of them.
   a. List and divide them—realistic from unrealistic.
   b. Goals to accomplish today—done every day.
   c. Next week.
   d. Long term, future goals.
4. What were my goals as a child?
5. What kept me from pursuing them?
6. Could I pursue them now if I chose to?

"We are what we confess" is a nice and flexible yardstick by which to enjoy your progress.

All day long I would discharge noises from my mouth—all supposedly designed to express my feelings to myself and the world at large. Since I didn't understand their meanings, let alone what I was feeling, I experienced a great deal of confusion that was legitimate.

184

I devised Card 3 to help me be more aware of key words and phrases that are very much a part of our vocabulary. Also, I personally like a reference point at which I can periodically see where my head is and redirect myself, if necessary.

Complete Card 3 with an open mind, and be as honest as possible. Think before you circle anything, making sure you first understand the word; then match the three corresponding feelings to those numbered.

For instance: At the present stage of your recovery, is imperfection *intolerable, a reason to hide, or a reality?*

Circle the feeling that most closely describes yourself. There are no correct answers, only honest evaluations that will help you see the direction you will want to move toward. The last column is my evaluations as seen from the perspective of a recovered bulimic.

You will have the opportunity to choose and match your feelings again.

Remember, *we are what we confess,* so go to your dictionary for clarification of the words, and to your heart for the cleansing honesty.

Card No. 3/We Are What We Confess

1. *Imperfection*	intolerable	a reason to hide	a reality
2. *To Purge*	get rid of calories	cleanse myself	panic out of guilt
3. *Isolation*	safety	lonely	danger
4. *Relief*	binging	purging	surrender
5. *Bulimia*	disgusting	temporary	challenging
6. *Failure*	lack of control	eating too much	not me!
7. *Forgiving Myself*	difficult	impossible	release
8. *Cry*	weakness	fear of exposing myself	allowance to feel
9. *Perfection*	thinness	realizing I don't have to be perfect	God
10. *Control*	to win	safety	let go, let God
11. *Stagnation*	frightening	better than taking chances	unacceptable
12. *Growth*	scary	I'd rather not	learning

13. *To Daydream*	a waste of time	sinful	productive planning
14. *Panic*	to binge	to show anger	confusion
15. *Confusion*	fearful	growth	derailment
16. *To Overeat*	comfort	to hide	to punish

Card No. 4/Cravings

1. Write the cravings down. What do you want?
2. The time of day or night.
3. The intensity on a scale of 1 to 10.
4. Try to bring the intensity down one point at a time.
5. Break the pattern by prolonging it, and forcing yourself to write what you are going to eat, when you are going to eat it, and what you are feeling when you crave, eat, and purge.

The purpose of Card 4 is to remove the mindlessness of the binge, and help waken you long enough to be more aware of what you're doing.

Card No. 5/Symptoms

Bulimia is a symptom of hiding our feelings. We have probably been finding ways and means to do this even in childhood. It is a striving for control in the only area we feel safe in doing so. Having withdrawn from growing emotionally at an early age meant we had other forms of the same symptoms. Try to remember how you managed to keep your feelings under wraps before the ultimate manifestation of bulimia. Also try to recall how you stopped one phase of denial and began another. When did you decide to use food as the next form of control?

Card No. 6/What Was Fun

1. What was fun as a child?
2. When did it cease to be fun, and why?
3. How did it feel to give it up?
4. What does it feel like now not to enjoy it anymore?

5. Could you enjoy it again if you allowed yourself to?
6. What is fun now?
7. How many *fun* diversions are there in your life?
8. Is there any guilt attached to them, and why?
9. Now let your imagination run rampant: What sounds like fun to you? See yourself doing it. Is it realistic fun, or just a dream? Could you make it a reality? Do you want to? What are other realistic ways to have fun, and what keeps you from pursuing them?

Card No. 7/What Is Fun

Sometimes the homework involved in pursuing fun isn't appealing. If you believed that finding ways to have fun would save your life, what present obstacles would you remove in order to insure your safety?

Fun is necessary and therapeutic; find yours and develop it. Make a conscious effort to discover more ways to enjoy life, have fun!

Card No. 8/How I Choose To Be Responsible Through a Bulimic Cycle

1. I recognize that a stressful situation exists.
    a. Any time I am hungry beyond hunger, I am reacting to a confusing stress that I have not as yet identified or found an alternative to.
2. Does the stress originate from an inner source, or an outer?
    a. Am I listening and believing a tape from the past?
    b. Have I allowed someone or something to trigger my stress?
    c. Both sources feel like they are controlling me and there is no way to fix it. I feel trapped. The only way to feel a release is to eat until the pain in my stomach is more than the pain I feel by not understanding my stress; then I punish myself for both pains by purging.
3. What are the alternatives to binging and purging?
    a. After understanding which source I am dealing with, I am now ready to assume the responsibility for an alternative to the binging and purging. Sometimes there is a release

187

when the source of the stress is identified; however, if not, I am willing to go further.

b. If I am listening and reacting to an old tape being played from the past, it is my option to go with it and binge and purge, or believe the truth, which is: *I am no longer a child and cannot be controlled by a fearful past. The tape I am listening to is a lie and I am capable of breaking its hold on me by choosing not to continue to believe it. I can reinforce this decision with Bible verses, prayer, and faith that the truth will set me free. If I had chosen to go with it, I would have been operating negatively to all of my positive qualities; not true to myself, but in exact opposition.*

c. If the stress is from an outside source, is it possible to change the effect of it by openly confronting it? If I do, how will the confrontation change or affect me or the others around me? Will I know the outcome beforehand? Do I anticipate that my truth will hurt someone? Will I expose a vulnerability that may be used against me now or later? Is the risk worth giving up the binge and purge for?

d. If I don't feel I can confront the stress openly, it is my responsibility to find a way to defuse the power of the outside source, not pout, become resentful, angry, or binge and purge. In other words, not allow my inability to confront the stress head on or to hurt myself or another.

4. If I am dealing with the real stress, I am too busy to binge!

Card No. 9/Just For Me

1. What is the most daring thing you have ever done? Something you wanted to do, not because it would be pleasing to someone else, or was expected of you—something daring only to you.
2. What do you want out of life? List your desires.
3. What would you like to accomplish, not to please anyone else, only you personally?
4. What really makes you happy—you alone?

Card No. 10/Responsibility

1. What does responsibility mean to me?
2. Is there one or more that frightens me?
3. Are there those I am consciously avoiding?

4. What keeps me from accepting them, and have I even faced them yet?
5. Are there any I have taken on that aren't necessary? If so, why? If I could take any one of them away, which one would it be?
6. Am I looking forward to being capable of handling more?

Card No. 11/Anger

1. As long as I harbor anger, I am crippling my ability to recover from my illness.
2. I now make the conscious decision to discover my true anger in order to determine how best to deal with it.
3. Once I am able to recognize and accept that I feel this anger, I will then be able to *defuse* its power to make me feel I am not in control of my feelings.
4. My assignment is to find alternative ways to deal with the now exposed *anger.*
5. There are always alternatives!
6. I will confront the causes of my anger, put them where they belong, and learn from them. In this way I will be redirecting their hold on my life, and I will be able to find relief from them.
7. I am now ready to list the causes of anger.

Card No. 12/Commitment

1. Do I fully understand the word commitment? What is my definition? What is the dictionary's definition? Compare.
2. How have I been applying the word to my condition?
3. List the drawbacks to the commitment of giving up bulimia or anorexia. (What would I lose by giving it up; would I have to face anything, or discover anything about myself?)
4. List the good reasons for giving it up.
5. Weigh the two lists. Are the good reasons worth the commitment? Do they outweigh the drawbacks that would have me continue to embrace bulimia or anorexia?

6. It is time to redefine my commitment, making sure my head and heart both want to recover sufficiently to withstand changes that might be forthcoming and uncomfortable at first.
7. I realize getting better often appears to be painful until I can see the light at the end of the tunnel. If I choose to continue and pursue my commitment, it proves that I know I am worth the effort, and I want to see the light at the end of the tunnel!

Card No. 13/Honesty

(You may want to pass on this one until you feel more confident.)
1. For two days a week (I will pick them) I will be honest in all things.
2. On these two days I will not binge or purge.
3. My honesty will make it easy to encourage my self-esteem, and make it no longer necessary to punish myself.
4. I will concentrate on the feelings that absolute honesty brings out in me.
5. I will pay close attention to the reactions of those affected by my honesty; however, I will not allow their reactions to deter me from my goal.
6. This goal is to find and develop my true nature, that of honesty and truth.
7. There is no guilt in honesty, only strength and self-esteem.
8. The truth has set me free!

Card No. 14/Strength (Starving Anorexia Only)

1. I can do all things with the strength that God gives me.
2. I want, and know that I *must* gain weight in order to learn more about myself.
3. I am a good person, and I want to learn to love myself.
4. By gaining weight, I will learn more and discover all the good things about myself that have been hiding.
5. The truth will set me free, and I welcome it.

Card No. 15/Control

1. To relax is to get well and prosper; to control is to stay sick and in despair.
2. I must try to loosen the control of the lower personality in order to accept my healing from God, through his insight and understanding, and then give the control back to God, where it belongs.
3. Perhaps I have been devoting my energies to controlling my feelings by not allowing myself the necessity of acknowledging any feeling—literally, *how it feels to feel.* This is *not* control; this is denial, regression, a lack of growth.
4. To validate this denial and lack of growth with my emotions, I have taught myself to tune them and other people out, while tuning in on the area that I think I can control—my body's intake and subsequent rejection of food.
5. This is a falsehood of the past, and can be corrected *because I choose to* correct it.
6. I now choose to give any control that is keeping me from progressing, back to God, and ask him to recycle it.
7. I trust that his will is not for me to go against the personality he has given me, but to enhance it, and become happier with myself.

Card No. 16/Confession

1. What I confess becomes the truth. This is why it is so important to confirm my affirmations every day; the truths must be played on my good tape long enough to be recognized as reality. When I confess I am growing and working my way through the trial, then the truth can truly set me free to enjoy blessed reality!
2. I confess that today I am growing and getting better!
3. I realize that like and love are separate feelings, and that in order to love myself, I must also like myself. Therefore, it is vital to discover my likable qualities and confess them in writing so that I can confirm them.
4. I confess that I like myself more and more every day.
5. I understand that my own self-love is a necessity to my recovery, and so I will love myself more and more.
6. It is impossible to love others until I am loving myself more; so I am eager to begin discovering my likable qualities and

191

confessing them. I am loving myself for them, and thanking God for helping me find and accept them for the truth. The truth has set me free!

Card No. 17/Pride

To be accused of being prideful is embarrassing and insulting—and I am immediately defensive. Is it possible that I am allowing, indeed *choosing* bulimia as a release and a means of not having to face the pride in my life? What is the difference between loving myself and being prideful? I had better find out!

There are several definitions of the word pride. The dictionary describes it as an exaggerated self-esteem, or a sense of one's own self-respect, or the delight in one's own achievements. The first definition sounds wrong; however, the next two do not. It is obvious that the word itself can be taken two ways. It is important to understand which definition I am applying to myself.

I am what I confess, and I want to be clear about what I am confessing. References in the Bible are: Mark 7:15-23; Proverbs 13:10; Isaiah 14:13-16; and Luke 18:11. These verses are quite clear. Therefore, perhaps it is time to examine my own understanding of pride and consider in what areas of my life I could benefit by choosing to eliminate it. To do so is to learn, grow, and discover another reason for not having to depend on bulimia as a release and a means to hide.

Is my sense of self-respect exaggerated? Does pride keep me from forgiving people, and, in the process, forgiving myself? Is it hard for me to say, "I'm sorry," and mean it? Is it easier to puff up rather than search for the truth behind others' motives, remembering that pride, not the binge itself, defiles me?

Card No. 18/Defuse

Dictionary: Fuse—a hollow tube filled with combustible material used for setting off an explosive charge.

Our explanation: Defuse refers to the learned process of tuning out our emotions, or turning off our feelings. The hollow tube used is our throats. We cram the combustible material with the explosive charge (food) down our throats. Think about that!

Dictionary's electrical usage: Easily melted material placed in a circuit as safeguard. If current becomes too strong, metal melts, thus breaking the circuit.

Our explanation: Our bruised and confused feelings are the easily melted material placed in the circuit—which is deep inside ourselves so that we don't have to face it. The current signifies not being able to cope successfully with these feelings and emotions. When this current becomes too strong, the struggle too much, our feelings explode and we binge and purge—thus breaking the circuit, relieving and releasing the pressure, again and again.

We use the word defuse quite a bit in connection with getting better, so it is good to understand its meaning in relation to our use, and our symptoms.

Every word, every situation, can be turned into something positive.

Dictionary: Fuse—to join by melting, to blend together—beautiful! We want to *let go and let God.* Also, uniting and merging, *higher* and *lower* for a more stable and realistic relationship with ourselves and God.

1. How can I defuse the volcano inside me?
2. How can I alleviate some of the pressure of my volcano until the defusement is more complete?
3. What Scripture verses can I claim to help me?
4. Psalm 143 will help guide me, and Psalm 142 will remind me that my refuge, God, will have the ultimate victory!

Card No. 19/Growth Through Confession

It is vital to grow through an uncomfortable feeling or past experience. I don't want the added burden that the feeling of futility brings. I want to view my discomfort times as trials through which to learn and grow. If I am aware of this at the onset, then my positive confession of growth will see me through. If, on the other hand, my confession is, "Oh, no, here I go again—another time to fail," the only thing I will gain is another guilt feeling to add to my notch. If I gather enough guilt feelings, they will outweigh my growth confessions.

My confession is to be ready for the uncomfortable periods in my life. To prepare for them in advance turns positive confession into a sword.

There is a formula. It's my choice.

Card No. 20/Full Affirmations

1. I want to be careful to put small amounts of food on my plate. Large quantities threaten my serenity, threaten the peace I feel within myself.
2. When eating, I am careful to consume what I am hungry for first. I believe my stomach fills very quickly. Again, I feel threatened if I think I have to eat everything offered to me. I want to make very sure that I feel *satisfied* with my *choices*.
3. I don't like the feeling that comes over me when I allow myself to be overwhelmed by huge amounts of food or responsibilities. I prefer the good feeling of choosing the amount of food I take in, and the amount of responsibilities I take on. Am I coping with them? Do I want to? If I am not satisfied with my ability to cope, I don't feel good about myself, and I am overwhelmed. Perhaps I have more choices in their acceptance than I am aware of. If so, I need to reexamine them and the control they exert over my life, thus enabling myself more choices.
4. I need and want more choices in the amount of responsibilities in my life, and in the amount of food in my life. I can always allow more later.
5. I like the feeling of being almost full. I like to be coping, and knowing I *could* cope with more—if I chose to. I could eat more, but I know food will reappear later. I could accept another responsibility, but I know the option to do so is always available to me when I choose it.

Card No. 21/Self-Esteem Versus Self-Worth

1. Write down everything that gives or allows you to feel self-esteem.
2. Now make a list of the duties or activities that produce self-worth.
3. Which list is more appealing?
4. Which requires more work?
5. Is it a control to have to work in order to feel self-esteem, self-worth?
6. Does that control feeling keep you from pursuing or attaining that worth?
7. Can you maintain esteem, or is it a constant struggle?
8. Can you maintain worth? Are you ever safe enough to enjoy it?

9. What have you learned? Is it threatening, encouraging, or just enlightening?
10. If the answer is threatening, then you need to explore ways to eliminate that threat; if enlightening, you have a good basis with which to begin; if the answer is encouraging, you're on your way to recovery.

Card No. 22/Hyper

In the car on the way home from work, or in the afternoon during your most stressful period, be conscious of slowing down. Begin breathing more deeply in a concentrated effort to relax. Now try to become aware of breathing in forgiveness for any wrongdoing that day, forgiving the higher for not meeting any expectations, unfulfilled or put off for the next day. Now exhale the guilt and pressure that build from the demands we place on ourselves and others. Inhale again. Exhale and give up the worry that won't help anyway.

This simple exercise will help reestablish the higher priorities, and encourage the lower to trust the higher with alternatives to the automatic control behavior of binging. It is important to leave the job or situation there. Learning to do this is a job in itself, but well worth it. Relaxing in a difficult situation is a learned response, just as the obsession over weight was learned. Only hopefully, relaxing is a much more productive endeavor.

Before beginning the breathing exercises, consider: *Did I fail myself in some way? Embarrass myself or someone else; make a mistake that makes it hard to forgive myself? Did someone hurt my feelings?* In other words, take inventory of the day, then begin the exercises. When in the situation, write these feelings down. Even when the mistakes or problems seem insurmountable, it is essential first to forgive, especially ourselves. Until we can face the guilt of doing wrong, we are not facing the feeling, therefore not offering any alternatives for the lower to choose from.

It feels good to recognize a feeling, identify it, and do something with it—especially if that something is an alternative to binging and purging.

Again, write down any problems or situations for which you are unable to find alternatives, for they are like thick walls. Think about them. Even if you can settle it only in your mind, it will still bring a good deal of relief and release for the lower. You'll be cutting down on the stress and pressure of having to perform the solution immediately. This will again release the pressure from your volcano in a more productive way. If you ferret out your true feelings, the lower will want to trust the higher for perhaps the first time. This will encourage her to want to merge more often, and more permanently. You have nothing to lose except the horror of binging and purging.

Card No. 23/Black and White? How About Gray?

I am aware that my rigid control behavior leaves very little room for alternatives or choices. In order to help me see that every situation has at least three other alternatives to my predetermined solution, I am going to look at my decisions more carefully, and search for those other choices. Even if my alternatives are bizarre or totally unrealistic, I will still write them down. It is only necessary for me to become open to ideas and to help free my mind from rigid thinking.

Without realizing it, my world has become a black and white one. I do not allow for gray, but I want to.

Below are examples of our black, white, and gray world. Each situation will be accessed and then categorized as much as possible for me to view just how I am perceiving my decisions, and how I can better perceive them in the future. I will try for as many gray decisions as possible.

Black	Gray	White
imperfection	growing	perfection
binging (controlling)	relaxing	control
wrong	alternatives	right

Example: I don't want to go somewhere. If I choose to believe I have no choice in the matter, that is black. If I choose to go, but am miserable, that is white and I hate the decision. If I choose to go, but also to come home in an hour, I am choosing gray. By choosing gray, I am more relaxed, and growing because I am learning that there are always alternatives. That is definitely gray.

Card No. 24/Time Well Spent

It is very beneficial to understand why you are doing what you are doing while you are doing it. What are you doing in between eating *besides not eating?* Even if working is the immediate response, is it a job you enjoy, a means to a paycheck, or just a filler until it's time to do something really worthwhile—eat!

If I am taking a class at night so that I won't be at home gorging and purging, I am saying that not eating is more important than this class. Without even realizing it, I am no longer interested in learning; it has become only a time filler . . . something being done to put off binging.

Yes, I do suggest finding ways to take your mind off of bulimia, but not as a permanent fix! Look for activities that you already do, or will want to do, more than eat or not eat.

I write because I love to write, not as something to keep my mind off of binging. But there was a time, early into my recovery, when I wrote as a therapy, and definite time filler. But I was aware when the filler became a love. Find your wants and loves as quickly as you can. If, for now, they are only fillers, be aware of their purpose and be on the lookout for real loves.

Discern, as best you can, which of your time slots are fillers, and which are genuine attempts to enjoy, or learn, or pursue self-esteem. This is all a part of waking up from binging and purging—filling the voids created when the symptoms of bulimia no longer satisfy.

Card No. 25/Fear

1. Acknowledge fear, the emotion. Name the fear itself.
2. Why am I feeling it?
3. What can I do, as an adult, to alter or change the feeling of fear? What are my alternatives?
4. What options do my alternatives give me to deal with the situation?
5. Release.
6. How can I learn from the experience? How can I grow?
7. Relief!

Love is the only emotion I was born with. Fear had to be learned. Anything I have learned, I can choose to correct. I will correct and make alternative commitments to change and grow.

197

Card No. 26/Growth

Whether or not to binge is my choice, and my choice alone. If I do, I am deciding, all by myself, to give permission to the child within to alleviate the volcano of feelings in a very negative and harmful manner. I am communicating to her that I cannot or will not offer her an alternative to her eruptions.

I am choosing not to be a responsible parent. I am sorry I have chosen to turn all responsibility over to my emotionally irresponsible child within myself.

To that child: *Please do not give up on me. I will genuinely try, through prayer, God's Word, and the tenacity he has given me ... to become the parent you need to help you grow up, and merge with me.*

I can do this by absorbing more truth and affirmations from God to help me grow stronger. 1 John 4:18 proves to me my need to grow and to believe, and that God's perfect love for me will eliminate all dread of what he might do to me. I want to accept his love so that I can then offer mine to you. I want to be able and desirous to offer you alternatives to binging and purging. You and I, as parent and child, have a desire and need to love one another and merge in that love.

His love enables me to rest and not be so afraid of my coming responsibilities with you, and for us.

Let's grow through God and look forward to the day when we believe in that growth to such an extent that neither of us will have to feel forced to *choose* binging or purging.

For further help with bulimia or anorexia nervosa, contact:

A.N.A.D.
Box 271
Highland Park, IL 60035

or

Jackie Barrile
Box 2351
Irwindale, CA 91706

YES, I am interested in further information on EATING AND FEELING DISORDERS.

Name_____ Phone_____

Address _____

City_____State_____Zip_____

Please send me more information on:
☐ Future seminars ☐ Workshops ☐ A seminar for my group or organization
☐ Textbook and tapes ($75.00) ☐ Newsletter ($5.00/year)
☐ Guided Imagery Tape ($12.95) ☐ Seminar Tapes ($15.00 for 2 tapes)

(CA residents add 6% tax. LA County residents add 6½% tax.)

Mail to

INNER DEVELOPMENT **P.O. Box 2351
Irwindale, CA 91706**

199